THE PEAR IS RIPE

First published in 2007 by
Liberties Press
Guinness Enterprise Centre | Taylor's Lane | Dublin 8 | Ireland
www.libertiespress .com
info@libertiespress.com
+353 (1) 415 1224

Trade enquiries to CMD Distribution
55A Spruce Avenue | Stillorgan Industrial Park | Blackrock | County Dublin
Tel: +353 (1) 294 2560
Fax: +353 (1) 294 2564

Distributed in the United States by
Dufour Editions | PO Box 7 | Chester Springs | Pennsylvania | 19425

and in Australia by
James Bennett Pty Limited | InBooks | 3 Narabang Way | Belrose NSW 2085

ISBN: 978–1–905483–25–9
Slipcased edition: ISBN: 978–1–905483–32–7

2 4 6 8 10 9 7 5 3 1

A CIP record for this title is available from the British Library

Liberties Press gratefully acknowledges the financial assistance of the
Arts Council in relation to the publication of this title.

Cover design by Liam Furlong at space.ie
Set in Garamond
Printed by Athenaeum Press | Dukesway | Team Valley | Gateshead | UK

THE PEAR IS RIPE

A MEMOIR

JOHN MONTAGUE

To all who marched in a good cause.
And to the future: Oonagh, Sibyl, Eve.

CONTENTS

PREFACE

The Pear Is Ripe, sequel to my first memoir, *Company or A Chosen Life*, moves between Berkeley, Paris and Ireland. It is a personal survey of sex and society through the 1960s and onwards, by someone who was lucky enough to travel between the major social and political flashpoints. The technique is revelation by anecdote, as practised by Elias Canetti: characters reappear, like Tom Parkinson, the Yeats scholar; Nelson Algren, the Chicago novelist; and Todd Andrews, the Irish commissar; as well as my New York hostess, 'Bananas' O'Rourke. And of course my first wife, Madeleine.

In *Company* I describe how, from the mid-fifties to the early sixties, Ireland began to open up to outside influences, through people of vision like Liam Miller of the Dolmen Press. That book also includes contrasting studies of Samuel Beckett and Brendan Behan, and the American poet Theodore Roethke, whom I introduced to Mrs Yeats. While my main interest is poetry, I have always admired the prose muse, in particular the artful ramblings of George Moore, and hope that my efforts may finally weave into a similar tapestry.

In the writing I have been helped by the professional skills of my novelist wife, Elizabeth Wassell, to the point where I am not always sure where my phrases end and hers begin. The title, however, comes from Flaubert's novel *L'Education Sentimentale*, which has the political events of 1848 as a background.

John Montague, Nice, July 2007

PART I

1

PARADISE REVISITED

OR TO CALIFORNIA THEN I CAME

> remembering powers of love
> and of poetry,
> the Berkeley we believed
> grove of Arcady –

Robert Duncan

When I came back to Berkeley for the spring semester of 1965, something had changed; a new electricity charged the air. The major reason was the Vietnam war, with troop ships and planes leaving for south-east Asia from the Bay Area: San Francisco, Oakland and the Alameda Naval Base. So my students would absent themselves from class for demonstrations: lying down on railway tracks before the troop trains, marching endlessly, and being hauled off to jail where I tried to visit them. That fine Californian poet Robert Duncan was kindled to a visionary, Blakean fury by this confrontation between a rigid society and its idealistic, ardent offspring:

> Now Johnson would go up to join the great simulacra
> of men,
> Hitler and Stalin, to work his fame
> with planes roaring out from Guam over Asia . . .

from 'Passages'

These were external factors; there were also internal aspects of the new revolutionary fervour, as, at long last, young America began to cut loose. The primary aspect of release was sexual: many of my students arrived at class looking rumpled and dreamy, but wreathed in smiles, as though they had spent the night making love, smoking pot, or, more likely, both. Still unaccustomed to the new mores, I found myself beside one of my youngest female students, who was dressed in the coy, little-girl style of the period – miniskirt and penny loafers – at the counter of the Wells Fargo bank. 'Who is the other name on your account?' asked the teller in a friendly fashion. 'That's my lover,' she said loftily. 'He's very good in bed.'

Suddenly, nobody wanted to appear innocent. Naivete had become decidedly uncool, virginity being the uncoolest state of all.

*

The English Department had also changed, even physically, shifting camp from the very functional Dwinelle Hall (with the exception of some lovely Chinese art, exquisite clay horses rearing inside glass cases) to the bulk of Wheeler Hall across the way. Wheeler was large and squat, with lifts rising between its broad floors. The departmental office was spacious, with its many professorial pigeonholes – or mailboxes – and the head of department encased behind glass and shielded by our wonderful secretary, Alyce Foley. This was the nerve centre of the English Department, only a short distance away from the bustle of Sather Gate, with its stalls and coffee stands, like a thronged Oriental market.

When I had stayed with tall Tom Parkinson and his diminutive wife, Ariel, in aloof Cragmont, I had walked or bussed down, past the Rose Garden, through the North Gate, and beneath the resounding Campanile. Now I had exchanged the responsibilities of a domestic life chez Parkinson for the freedom of the small, dingy Carlton Hotel (their hotel stationery described it modestly: 'Only one block from Main Entrance to the University of California, Berkeley's most convenient location.') It was louche, forlorn and strange in a peculiarly American way, conjuring up the stories of Carson McCullers or Nelson Algren, or the thrillers of Dashiell Hammett.

Soon such establishments would be supplanted by glossy motels, but I was lucky enough to experience the Carlton in all its tawdry glamour. Its residents included a frail old woman who would give me a leprechaun on my birthday, a number of shipwrecked salesmen, and a few small-time gamblers, although there was also a section for students, which was somewhere at the back. I wrote to Madeleine: 'This is my new location, a wide room with a small view of the Bay. For sixty bucks a week I get "maid service", which sounds beautiful, but simply means that a black lady cleans my room when I ain't in it. Indeed, chastity is the order of the day, as NO MIXED VISITORS are allowed.'

I strolled up past Cody's bookshop, along Telegraph Avenue, with its aromas of spice and coffee, and, increasingly, something stronger. Both outside and inside Sather Gate, students were discussing, disputing, lofting banners, chanting slogans, and beating gourd drums. After the torpor and docility of the fifties, everything was suddenly up for scrutiny and challenge, with leaders like Mario Savio striding among their followers like film stars. Images of campus sixties radicalism have become a cliché now, but in those days it was still astonishing to see such political fervour among the young, the like of which had probably not existed since 1848, when small sparks of rebellion had kindled fires all over Europe.

Later in the year, I would grow weary of this warm bath of political passion and personal excess, with my students trying LSD and losing their previous fiery edge, their grades dropping as they dropped acid; but in the beginning it did seem splendid. The crowds swirled and spilled onto the broad steps of Wheeler Hall, where more groups would eddy and coalesece before passing into the formal seriousness of the lecture halls, where the hubbub would gradually die down. (Later, the need for confrontation would roughen the relationship between student and teacher to near breaking point.)

I had inherited the office of an American-Irish expert on Irish literature, Brendan Ó hEithir, who had left for Ireland on a sabbatical. He had the same name as another writer friend of mine from Galway, a nephew of the fierce Liam O'Flaherty, and I felt intellectually at home amid his books, as though I were in a library room in Ireland – despite the lush Californian foliage outside the window. Brendan was working on the Gaelic references in *Finnegans Wake*, and Tom Parkinson, in his study above, was continuing to decipher the handwriting of Yeats' manuscripts. Between them, I felt like a ship in a green bottle.

My room had two desks, a large one and a small one, as well as, strangely enough, a capacious broom closet. What a contrast my temporary quarters made with those of my comrade, Gary Snyder, downstairs! Gary had installed a tatami prayer mat and some delicate bonsai trees in the corner he had set aside for meditation. And there were scrolls on the walls – misty scenes of mountains and birds, recalling the visionary paintings of Morris Graves. Gary's attitude towards his students was different from, and complementary to, mine: he was interested in their spiritual progress, and the need to develop a discipline of contemplation from which poetry might be distilled. He had inherited some of my students from the previous year's poetry workshop, and spoke enthusiastically of one, saying he was a real seeker. I wanted to improve their poems, while he was concerned with them as pilgrims, aiming to improve their souls so as to improve their verses.

So Gary and I seemed to balance each other well, and were almost foils for each other. I have always enjoyed working with others, and try not to be a prima donna unless it is necessary to keep the show going. Besides, I was increasingly impressed by the variety of Gary's skills. He had spent most of the previous decade in Japan, and was fluent in conversational Japanese, as well as translating from the Chinese and practising its marvellous calligraphy. Tom Parkinson described Snyder with his usual acuity: 'There is a physical, intellectual and moral sturdiness in him that is part of each movement he makes and each sentence he phrases. He is gracious, soft-spoken, incisive and deeply intelligent. He is also an extraordinarily skilful poet. . . . If there has been a San Francisco renaissance, Snyder is its renaissance man: scholar, woodsman, guru, artist . . . accessible, open and full of fun.'

As well as appreciating each other's very different work and enjoying each other's company, Gary and I agreed that working in the English Department at Berkeley was no sinecure. In addition to a master class, I taught a bigger workshop, which swelled in number until I had to seek two teaching assistants, one of whom, David Bromige, was a poet himself, a young Englishman enamoured of the New Poetics of Robert Creeley and Charles Olsen. Gary and I also had to take on a first-year Shakespeare class; mine was crowded with youthful political activists. After my troubled affair with a black-haired colleague the year before, I had become obsessed with the mystery of the Dark Lady sonnets: 'If snow be white, why then her breasts are dun:/ If hairs be wires, black wires grow on her head . . . '. I would urge my students to take the slim volume with them to anti-war rallies, or even to jail. 'I have seen roses damask'd, red and white/ But no such roses see I in her cheeks . . . ' struck me as suitable lines for a sunless prison. Unfortunately, my incarcerated students were inclined to confrontation rather than reading and reflection.

After all this teaching, and the attendant student-teacher conferences demanded by the administration, there were the innumerable quizzes, reports and term papers. By Friday, Gary and I were as grumpy as overburdened office clerks or factory workers; had Kenneth Rexroth, the daddy of the San Francisco renaissance, not described Berkeley as 'a Ford factory of the intellect'? So I would accompany Gary to his San Francisco pad for some relaxation. It made a marvellous contrast to climb onto the back of his big, glittering motorcycle, and surge across the Bay, leaving our academic selves behind. Gary's pad was in North Beach, under the phallic presence of the Coit Tower, and across the way from the city's favourite intellectual hangouts, the City Lights Bookshop and the Vesuvio Café. It was already a different North Beach from the one I had enjoyed the previous year with Parkinson – more free and open, but with its own peculiar disciplines and rituals. We would shed our academic gear at Gary's Green Street studio and then set out to explore the local scene.

The little hill under the Coit Tower was swarming with young people in pursuit of learning and pleasure. They seemed to be mainly rich young women from Southern California, long-legged girls nourished on orange juice – though now they had advanced to wine and, of course, pot and other mild drugs. Gary seemed to know them all, but our visits to their flats were not occasions of pure excess, despite our eagerness to unwind, because the young women were searching in their own way. There was something ritualistic even in the taking of the wine, which was Mountain Red poured from big jugs, and of course the sharing of the joint afterwards was as ceremonial as the passing of a Native American peace pipe.

Gary was a born teacher who never missed an opportunity to raise the level of consciousness of his company. So we discussed the city that lay beneath us, Chinese and Japanese poetry, languages and linguistics. Gary's intellectual and spiritual focus was always sharp, in spite of the drink and drugs; perhaps it was even heightened by them. After these few quiet hours on some-one's terrace, watching the sky darken as the sun went down over San Francisco, we moved off separately or in groups to one or other of the cheap Italian restaurants of North Beach, our appetites whetted by the pot we had smoked. The New Pisa was still there from my graduate-student days, and the Old Spaghetti Factory, which was crammed at night with long-haired men and women, the ur- or proto-hippies. Afterwards we sorted our-selves out for the night, in the casual way of that time and place, either coupling, or crashing into bed alone.

I gawped happily at all this, pleased to be let into this world that was at once hedonistic and rigorously disciplined. But the little Ulster Catholic boy inside me still blanched when Gary's ideas of collective ritual extended to sex. In his liberal yet strict view, even lovemaking was a discipline, and he encouraged me to let go of my Irish hang-ups and participate in communal sex, which he argued would liberate me – though I wondered how one could be a monk of the erotic? He explained that when he had been blocked in his second and perhaps most beautiful book, *Myths & Texts*, he had worked his way clear with 'secret, frantic rituals' of drugs and sex, which had lowered the boom:

> I have terrible meditations
> On the cells all water
> > frail bodies
> Moisting in a quiver;
> Flares of life that settle
> Into stone
> The hollow quaking of the soft parts
> Over bone

from Myths & Texts (1960)

17

It was a friendly rivalry between us, with me blaring Yeats and Auden to him, the structured poetry of Europe and the East Coast, and Gary telling me to loosen up. Yet I never ceased to be astounded by the paradoxes in his attitude: he would chasten me for being 'uptight' and 'hung up', and would exhort me to take part in orgies, but his sense of discipline was so stern that it was nearly puritanical. And it was astonishing how much scholarship could be applied to everything, even sex and drugs, especially natural drugs like 'Morning Glory'. According to the myth, Morning Glory dated back to pre-Colombian Mexico, where it had been used by the Nahuatl Indians, and supposedly the Native Indians in Oaxaca were still taking it. The students and seekers discoursing solemnly on it sounded like botanists as they recited the names of species and genera, *rivea corymbosa* and *ipomea*, applying an earnest pedantry to the sybaritic and the sensual. 'You're not an Indian, or a Zen Buddhist from Japan. You're a trim Dutchman, with that Van Dyck beard,' I told Gary once, after he had yet again accused me of being 'an uptight, prudish Irishman' – which, indeed, I partly was. (I was also more or less a European, who found this systematic exploration of the erotic mysteries distinctly American. Also American, it seemed to me, was the absence of the personal, the romantic, in these sexual adventures. You engaged in them for self-improvement; love was not the point.)

Besides, after the previous year's turbulent affair, I was not eager to plunge back into the 'dark mysteries', and so I became quite friendly with Kimberly, a typically fair-haired, wholesome-looking young woman from Los Angeles, although her all-American good looks were hidden under a bushel, as it were, by a motorcycle and bomber jacket. She was a great fan of Gary, and her cultivation of the motorcycle was partly a homage to him, but also part of the culture of the period, from Brando's *The Wild Ones* onwards. Every weekend, groups of young black men thundered into Berkeley on their Harley-Davidsons, Hondas and Yamahas, to link up with high-school girls high on marijuana. Looking glamorous yet menacing, the bikers called themselves 'bloods', but did little damage except to themselves. And of course the cult film of the period was *Scorpio Rising*, a study of a brutish motorbike gang by Kenneth Anger, the author of *Babylon Revisited*. He had been a disciple of Aleister Crowley, and passed on Crowley's wand to Robert Duncan in a kind of magical succession.

Since Gary was this young woman's guru or master, he dictated her reading list and her yoga practices but did not seem to wish to take their relationship further, even though he was living alone at the time. In addition to Gary's wisdom, she had her own areas of expertise, and was a devotee of Morning Glory. In an unconscious parody of an efficient housewife, she would say: 'The best way to take it is to soak the seeds until their shells get soft, which makes them easier to chew.' Or: 'Grind up the seeds and mix them with water so that they form a kind of gruel. You can mix this into food or eat it on its own.'

As a Catholic, I loved the names of these potent seeds, which Kimberly intoned like a litany. Flying Saucers, Wedding Bells, Summer Skies and Blue Star suggested the various stages of hallucination, with Heavenly Blue and Pearly Gates the zenith. She said they were on sale in most Bay Area nurseries, and she always had a stack handy. But she allowed us to 'turn on' only after we had eaten a meal, and did not encourage drinking at the same time. Altogether she was as bustling and gentle as a housemother, administering her potions. Nor did she seem overly concerned with sex, although she was once so hurt when Gary seemed to be ignoring her that she slapped him.

Kim despised Berkeley and its conventional scholarship, preferring to search for wisdom within the new offbeat culture of American Indian lore, hallucinogens and Eastern religions. This arrangement suited me, because I preferred not to get too close-ly involved with students on the campus, even though Kim and I were really pals more than anything else, enjoying each other's easy companionship. She seemed to me, in her black leather trousers, a kind of modern Calamity Jane, hanging out with the boys. Another North Beach poet pal, the buckskin-clad Lew Welsh, thought she was probably lesbian. 'But,' he said coarsely, 'her balls haven't dropped yet.'

O Rose, Thou Art Sick, Part One

Artists discover offbeat areas and transform them into loci of defiant energy, only to be displaced by middle-class voyeurs with too much spare money – rendering these little meccas too expensive for those who created them. I believe I was lucky enough to savour North Beach life before the tourist invasion destroyed it, as it had previous bohemian centres like Montmartre. The old-fashioned bump-and-grind striptease of the International Settlement, where students and sailors mingled, would be replaced by go-go dancers – often with inflated silicon breasts, making them look as glossily artificial as Barbie dolls – suspended in cages. Whereas our North Beach scene was relatively sweet and harmless, with a serious note of self-exploration underneath.

And the flower children were still in bud; a year or so later, the kids would stream into Haight-Ashbury singing:

> If you're going
> to San Francisco
> Be sure to wear
> some flowers in your hair . . .

And the air would be full of their favourite music, the contralto voice of Grace Slick of Jefferson Airplane, the young Grateful Dead, the dove-like, soprano warblings of Joan Baez. But the first flower child I met was in my own large writing workshop at Berkeley – though I hardly noticed her at first – a short-skirted, chubby-faced child from Florida, with bright, scrubbed cheeks and an absurdly endearing name like something out of the *Canterbury Tales*: Rose Twirlaleaf.

I was beginning to become aware that several of my students were seriously dropping acid, and I was trying to deal with this new phenomenon with the help of 'guru' Gary, who had obviously had more experience with hallucinogens than me. Their trips were sometimes extreme: once I was called from my hotel to restrain a young man from jumping out of his window, since, he told us serenely, 'Space has dissolved, man.' I suppose I should have followed them in order to understand their experience first-hand, but laboratory hallucinogens alarmed me, as did the length of an LSD trip. A profound alteration of consciousness, lasting twelve or so hours, did not appeal to an Irishman like myself, who was only beginning to understand the relatively milder effects of social drinking on the body and mind.

I tried to make it a rule that students of mine who were taking LSD should write something before, during and after their trip, but rarely got anything satisfactory – certainly nothing like Gary's beautiful poems. I gathered that, during an LSD trip, objects achieved an almost mystical significance, but what came through in my students' writings was a microscopic attention to the most minute detail: one gave me a mini-thesis on a doorknob. In a way, their investigation of space, time and the basic structure of matter seemed to echo the concerns of my physicist friends like Charles Cattell, but were too fragmentary to serve as more than reports. Tom Flanagan, a fellow Berkeley teacher and a future novelist, thought it absurd that I absorbed myself so much in the psychic and political lives of my students. But then I was living downtown amongst them, and I had the example of Parkinson and Snyder, who were admired by many of the student leaders.

It was a big department and I got along with most of my colleagues, who were content that Gary and myself should deal with the more offbeat types. But gradually I began to sense a change in the attitude of the other English lecturers towards me.

When I passed them in the corridors of Wheeler, they would suppress a smile, or throw me a half-amused, half-wry look, which I could not read easily. Parkinson came to the point, bluntly: 'John, who has been decorating your door with flowers? Some of the older profs are starting to talk. You know what they're like: you can't afford to get the reputation of messing around with students, girls or boys. Clean up your act.'

I vaguely knew what he was talking about. Once or twice I had noticed flowers scattered on the floor outside my office, but the cleaners went round towards the end of morning lectures. So I took to coming in early, after a morning coffee at the Mediteranneum, and, yes, there was a garland, or daisy chain, draped over my doorknob, with a few extra blossoms on the noticeboard which advertised my office hours and other serious information. Fascinated, I arrived one morning shortly after the janitor had opened the big doors, and lay in wait down the corridor. And sure enough, I caught the miscreant, a smiling Rose Twirlaleaf, her arms festooned with flowers, like a chubby version of a Botticelli nymph. I confronted her as she was in the act of hanging a daisy chain over the door handle.

'Oh, Professor Montague,' she cried gaily, 'you've caught me out. I wanted to remain a secret admirer.'

Remembering Parkinson's injunction, I tried to appear as stern as possible, yet her cradled flowers kept drifting to the floor, and as I knelt to help her gather them up, our heads would bump disconcertingly. I threw a quick glance down the antiseptic corridor, but it was still early and there were no academic snoops yet. The cleaners would soon be coming by, though.

'Do you always do this for your professors?' I asked, severely.

'I always did it in high school, in Florida, but most of my teachers were women, and they loved flowers. I forgot you were a man.' She smiled – archly, I thought.

'Are there any other professors you honour in this fashion?'

'Gee, you speak like a book. That's why we all like your class. It's like being inside a British — sorry — *Irish* novel. Anyway, what's wrong with giving you a few flowers? I also bring them to my professor in Classics, but he's an old guy.'

And in conclusion, she declared what would soon become the anthem of the flower children, though at this point I had never heard it before: 'Flowers are symbols of peace and love, and love is the only power against the atom bomb.' Then, with her cheeky grin: 'And you poets should love symbols.'

I was defeated, but something had to be done. I swept her into my office and, exploring the contents of the big broom closet, found an ancient, dusty vase, which I gave to her. I explained that I would contrive to have the door opened every morning so that she could bring in the flowers and arrange them prettily in the vase; that way, I could breathe in the bouquet as I interviewed students or corrected term papers. 'Maybe your flowers will make my marking less severe.'

As I prepared to go down to my next class, where her smiling face would once again tilt up at me (wearing, from now on, a ghostly wreath of flowers), she explained how she gathered her copious garlands. 'I know nobody up here in Berkeley, so I'm pretty lonely. But I love the Berkeley Hills, and I go up there every morning, past the Bevatron and Strawberry Canyon. And there are whole clumps of wild flowers up there, so I sit there and braid them, and look down on the city and the Bay, and it all feels nice, and I love everybody, even though I don't know them.'

Only a year before, a reactionary fanatic had blundered into Parkinson's office brandishing a gun, with which he had blasted off part of Tom's jaw. I thought of this potential murderer sitting up in the same hills as Rose, cradling a rifle on his knees instead of flowers, and dreaming of clearing the campus of 'commies and homos' – and probably innocents like Rose as well. This vast, lovely landscape seemed to nourish such extreme dreams, which clashed against each other. On the one hand, there was a murderous maniac descending on the campus with Biblical zeal, an idealist in his own warped way, brandishing his shotgun like the sword of an avenging angel; on the other, flower children like Rose would soon be nestling daisies into the barrels of National Guardsmen's guns as part of their passive resistance to the Vietnam war. In a way, this had always been the story of America; I was uneasily beginning to wonder which side would prevail this time.

*

I thought I had nipped this *Roman de la rose* in the bud, as it were. Comment certainly died down in the department – so much so that Parkinson complimented me on my discretion. 'I want to get you back here full-time, Montague,' he said. 'So you must behave like a house-trained poet. You can do anything you want in North Beach, but you've got to keep your big nose clean on campus. Especially because everyone will be comparing you to our two English imports, Cox and Box.'

He was referring to two brilliant young English critics, Brian Cox of the *Critical Quarterly* and Manchester University, and Christopher Ricks from Oxford, who, from their very different perspectives, were sharing the Berkeley experience as visiting professors. (Although, fascinatingly, they did not seem to speak to each other, as though they could not exchange a salute before receiving the formal introductions of an older, quainter England. Eventually, I would ask Cox why he had not befriended his fellow Englishman – to which he replied regretfully: 'It's up to Ricks, you see. He's from Oxford.') I myself would become friendly with both, especially Brian, who was easy and open, eager to learn about the Bay Area poets, and even to publish them, particularly Snyder, after the advocacy of his work by Thom Gunn and myself.

Cox and Ricks had come to California with their families, and lived in faculty housing – not a ramshackle hotel like the Carlton. While I was enjoying the footloose freedom of my peculiar new life, observing my fellow transatlantic scholars reminded me that I, also, had attachments at home. In a letter, I gave Madeleine a discreet account of my adventures in North Beach, and she replied with a pithy French rhyme that was uneasily appropriate: 'Fruits sans saveur/ Femmes sans pudeur/ C'est la Californie'.

She seemed sure that nothing I might discover in this New World could make it match the Old. She could not imagine that the Berkeley she envisaged, full of wholesome, naive students, might threaten our life together, and she seemed untroubled by our long separation. In fact, she was full of plans for a French conference in Los Angeles, during which she hoped to come to Berkeley. She presumed that we could take up where we had left off, although for me a distance was growing between us which was not only geographical. After all, the currency of a couple's intimacy is their daily life together, and our day-to-day experiences were now so different, as well as so distant, from each other. I had had a kind of desolate vision as I flew west from Chicago (where I had halted briefly to see Nelson Algren), gazing down as the plane glided over the Mississippi and its tributaries:

> Flying from Chicago, I awake
> To see the Mississippi, spread-
> Eagled with its tributaries,
> A stricken tree of ice.
>
> For a moment its chill glitter recalls
> All that we had feared:

'The growing distances between
Our two lives . . .'

All in all, I was still trying to hold my various lives together.
Soon after I had arrived in Berkeley, and before my North Beach
days, I wrote hopefully to Madeleine: 'I have just discovered that
the men's swimming pool is open, so I will probably add that to
my schedule of peace and work and chastity!' But, perhaps significantly, the postcard showed a caged lion gazing gloomily
through the bars.

*

After placating Miss Twirlaleaf and her desire to offer floral
homage to the powers of poetry, I thought the balance between
my academic life in Berkeley, my off-stage life in North Beach,
and my distant French married life was secure. Indeed, I was
almost beginning to congratulate myself on my adroit juggling
of lifestyles, when there was a further twist. Partly due to her
detestation of the place, it was more or less agreed between
myself and Kimberly that she would not visit me on campus. So
I was surprised one day, coming up from one of my workshops,
to see her striding along through Wheeler Hall, looking healthy
and incongruous in her formidable motorcycle gear, like a Norse
goddess, with her fair hair standing out against the black leather
and metal. But she was walking away from, not towards, my
office; puzzled, I called after her. To my surprise, she turned an
angry face in my direction and shook her shining helmet at me,
before plunging down the stairs. I thought I heard 'Fuck off!'
float towards me from the depths of the stairwell. I hoped she
had not been heard or seen by my more busybody colleagues.
But what was wrong?

I settled wearily at my office desk, and began to correct a
new clutch of student compositions. Everything seemed in
place, undisturbed, so what could have upset Kimberly so

much? All she had to do was either wait outside or, since the door was open, come in and relax until the imminent end of class. Then I heard a scuffling noise, and what sounded like a series of muffled giggles. The place was empty, the door shut, so was I hallucinating, despite not having taken my Morning Glory recently? Perhaps it was actually a bird, since the voice I thought I'd heard had now begun to twitter and make strange warbling sounds. I peered through the window at the campus, as colourful and busy as a street in India, but there was no bird serenading me from the sill. Then, on a sudden inspiration, I whipped open the broom closet. Standing inside was none other than a flushed Rose Twirlaleaf, hand on mouth, eyes watering from the effort of suppressing her giggles.

'Were you making bird sounds?' I asked, accusingly. 'And did you hear somebody else come in?'

'I had been practising bird calls and I was hoping to surprise you. That other girl didn't seem to like them very much, but she doesn't look as if she's into birds or flowers. Where did you find her? She looked pretty scary to me.'

It took me weeks to calm Kim down, and I forbade Rose from bringing any more flowers to my altar. Some of these kids were just too much to handle, I thought.

A Pride of Poets, Part One

The most formidable presence in the poetic community of the Bay Area was Robert Duncan. I had just missed meeting him when Madeleine and I returned to Europe in 1956; indeed, I think we were hijacked by the then-director of the more sedate San Francisco Poetry Center, to prevent us from going to hear him speak on poetry and homosexuality. I suppose they thought this was not a subject that would interest a young heterosexual couple about to be married. But I was interested, because some of the most brilliant members of my generation at University College Dublin were homosexual, and I wanted to understand their world better.

I finally met Robert at a party given by a French-Canadian gallery owner called Paule Anglim, who was living in a splendid house in Marin County, just over the Golden Gate Bridge, the lights of which you could see, flashing from her long French windows. Robert's style of dress was as magnificent as the setting. He was sporting a swirling, poetic cloak, and a crimson waistcoat, and his good eye gleamed as he talked endlessly, wonderfully. Paule had arranged for us to be picked up in North Beach, and on the way out to her house we fell into an argument about whether animals could experience love. I was contending that dogs only rutted, and were not capable of tender feelings for each other. As we came through Paule's dramatic portals, a black guard dog leaped towards me, just missing my cheek. 'You see,' cried Robert, 'our so-called dumb friends can speak! He heard what you said, and was offended by your slight to the dog-god Anubis!'

Being with Robert was heady; he was the first poet I had met who lived and talked poetry like a religion, and for whom all the gods were still real. And then he came across the Bay from his San Francisco home, to speak in a seminar on Yeats that Parkinson and I had arranged. His deep, visionary eye, with shadows scalloped beneath, and the tufts of hair around his handsome, sallow face, made him resemble some mythological bird. Or the Ancient Mariner, as he discoursed on Yeats' *A Vision*, Yeats' mystic marriage with Maud Gonne, and his mediumistic relationship with his wife, George. It was the first time I had heard such things taken seriously, even in Dublin, although when I had walked to the university as a very young man, I had passed the headquarters of the Dublin Spiritualist Society. Tom Flanagan had spoken, with a novelist's fascination, of the complex strands of Yeats' lineage, and Walter Starkie had discoursed on his affinity with the poet García Lorca's use of the gypsy ballads, but Robert stole the show with his passionate belief in the magical as the very essence of great poetry. Not until I met Ted Hughes would I experience that same unshakeable belief in the mystical powers of poetry and art.

At the time I met him, Robert was on a roll, with three books having been published in quick succession, and to great critical acclaim: *The Opening of the Field* (1960), *Roots and Branches* (1964) and his ever-expanding *Bending of the Bow*, which would appear in 1968. And of course, in the background, there was the enormous, unfurling vision of his 'H.D.' book, as crammed with dreams, alchemy and magic lore as the wilder shores of Coleridge. There was something flamboyant and flagrant about Robert's personality and poetry, 'the poet in a frenzy, with his fine eye rolling', in a way that seemed more acceptable in California than on the East Coast. Or indeed than in the American South: when James Dickey came to read in Berkeley, I brought him over to see Robert and his boyfriend Jess in their strange surroundings, with plump cats lolling beneath Jess's eerie paintings, which combined a kind of super-realism with childlike fantasy. It seemed to me, coming from Yeats' Dublin, like the heady atmosphere of a late-Romantic household. But Jim Dickey found the same atmosphere stifling – inimical to his macho sensibility. 'It's not an air I can breathe,' he wrote to me afterwards.

O Rose, Thou Art Sick, Part Two

Meanwhile, things were hotting up back at the academic ranch. The FSM, or Free Speech Movement, was burgeoning on campus, and soon numbered over ten thousand people, committed to challenging the assumptions of their society. But students are playful, and a young man called, I think, John Thompson (although, under the circumstances, he could just as easily have been called John Thomas), paraded across the campus with a sign reading 'FUCK'. When the cops busted him for obscenity, he explained that, if he had sauntered around with a sign saying 'WAR' or 'KILL', it would have been quite acceptable and legal. Clearly a young man with a strong sense of humour, he confessed that 'My mother forced me to do it', but then retracted that statement, declaring instead: 'It was the Pope.'

To taunt the Berkeley administration further, a sympathiser with John Thompson (or Thomas) called Michael Kline was trying to raise money to bail out John and pay his legal costs. But when Kline and his companions were arrested as well, for sitting at their table and collecting 'bread' for the Defense Fund, he began to declaim selected passages from *Lady Chatterley's Lover* which flaunted the 'F' word. The edition he used, which had a preface by Mark Schorer of the Berkeley English Department, was confiscated by the police, and I imagined a crowd of burly men in blue avidly reading the 'dirty' bits in their station house. Perhaps we should have sent them copies of Mike McClure's poem, reclaiming the 'F' word:

> It was fucking quiet.
> The fucking flower of silence breathes its fucking air.

I was so fucking high, I trembled.
Oh fuck, fuck, fuck, shatter me and lift me free.
The night was fucking long.
Oh fuck, oh honest word oh.

The politics of it all became very complicated since the FSM disapproved of the 'Fuck Affair', maintaining that it was the kind of callow trap students habitually fall into. 'Trying to build some kind of movement around the word "fuck" . . . at a time when our government is slaughtering innocents . . . is a cop-out on the real movements for freedom,' according to Mike Myerson of the DuBois Club. Myerson explained further: 'What is really obscene is Dallas County Sheriff Jim Clark bull-whipping black Americans, or President Johnson napalming Indochinese.'

Then the administration made a startling move, with both the president and the chancellor of the university resigning in a dramatic display of disgust at the 'Fuck Controversy'. 'Strategically,' I wrote to Madeleine, 'their object is to discredit the whole political activity on the campus by fastening on the most absurd aspect of it.' Such confrontation had been coming for a while. The Chaucer scholar Charles Muscatine (who was presumably an expert on bawdy language) and Parkinson were sympathetic to the students, yet for a while even they had been pleading with them to 'cool it' and to 'stop rocking the boat'.

But the students were on a roll. To the background noise of the pounding of drums on the campus, like the heartbeat of revolt, they strolled from stall to stall and speaker to speaker, in a kind of youthful version of Hyde Park Corner. And they had already attracted a lot of outside attention, from both the Left and the Right. Conor Cruise O'Brien came to speak against the war in Vietnam in Sproul Plaza, in front of the Admissions Office. Conor and I went drinking afterwards in the home of a

South African friend of mine, where Conor spouted Yeats like a Berkeleyan fountain.

Crossing the campus one day, I glimpsed the slender figure of the highly conservative English poet Robert Conquest, accompanied, as usual, by a stylish young woman. Bob seemed uncomfortable at seeing me, and would not answer my delighted query: 'What brings *you* here?' Only later did the penny drop: had I not grown used to calls at my office from clean-shaven, crisp-suited young men enquiring about the moral character of this or that student, because, the young men hinted solemnly, they were being considered for 'an important governmental task'? Considering the films and TV series about spies and 'secret agents' that were proliferating at the time, it wasn't hard to figure out what those sober young men meant. In any case, the Right had its eye on the Left, and the Left was flaring in all directions, like fireworks.

Yet office hours at Berkeley were still pretty serious, with students discussing their papers, stories or poems as if they were products of flying genius, when they clearly had, as yet, very little to write about beyond their insulated backgrounds. Rose Twirlaleaf had decided that she was a poet and, alas, that I was her muse, being not only a writer, but exotic — coming from a faraway place and speaking with a strange accent. And with a confidence that was at variance with her childish appearance, she set out in pursuit of me.

(I had in fact already experienced this phenomenon: in the new, exhilarating climate of political radicalism and free love, some of my students seemed to be confusing the classroom with the bedroom. A young woman in my poetry workshop wrote verses extolling a beautiful female body, and when I asked her, during office hours, whether the body had been inspired by a painting, she replied tranquilly: 'No, it's my own. Would you like to see it?' I managed to rebuff most such offers, despite the fact that, in those days, teacher-student love affairs were becoming par for the course. Due to my remote but very real life back in Paris, and my own personal confusions, I was still ambivalent about such approaches.)

I had been trying to dampen Rose's enthusiasm towards me for some time: my refusal of her floral tributes had not cooled her ardour. Only occasionally would I take a coffee with her and her Classics teacher, an old gent who was clearly delighted by her seemingly childlike appetite for life, and kept making comparisons between the youth of Berkeley and the youth of Sparta, and invoking Virgil's Golden Age!

One day after class, a troubled-looking Rose said that she had something serious to discuss with me, beyond the workshop assignments. Could I give her a special office hour? I sat, astounded, as she described what she said was the central problem of her life, which might lead to her withdrawing from the university. 'You know, Professor Montague, it may be hard for you to understand, coming from so far away, but I'm really different from everyone else on this campus. Everyone in Berkeley is so hip and with-it; they don't seem to have any problem with sex. I believe that I'm the only virgin around, and if I told anybody, they'd just scream with laughter. So I've come to the conclusion that you, as my Virgil and poetic mentor, should help me with this dilemma. According to my Classics teacher, it was a practice in some older cultures for the elders to initiate the young into the Mysteries. It seems to me that it is your obligation to release me from the burden of ignorance.'

As I stared, dumbstruck, she concluded – with a blithe, even brutal practicality which was in sharp contrast to her invocation of the Eleusinian Mysteries – 'Besides, you're going back to Europe soon, so you wouldn't talk. And I'll tell nobody, you can bet on that.'

It took me a moment to gather my wits, and shoo Rose out

of my office. 'An office hour,' I told her sternly, 'is for discussion of students' work, and not their private life.'

'But one depends on the other!' she wailed, disappearing down the corridor, uncomfortably like Kimberly before her.

*

Rose began to haunt me – though not, I hasten to say, because her daft proposition had enkindled me with desire. Her curious plea had flustered me into considering her real position in Berkeley, and was exciting in me not lust, but a kind of rueful pity. I even had a dream in which a calf, with Rose's doleful eyes, was being brought to a sacrificial pyre, its head festooned with a wreath of white roses.

It seemed to me that America, or at least California, was becoming a vast sexual laboratory, where surgeon and patient were equally ignorant, and where matters were not leavened by tenderness; and that in this new, very tolerant atmosphere, Rose seemed extremely vulnerable, despite her evident boldness. Apolitical, and dressed in the mawkish style of those days – when grown women were compelled to wear gymslips and cultivate a doe-eyed look – she gave me the impression of being nearly always alone. The students seemed perpetually to surge across the campus in groups, either political or social, but where were Rose's friends? Was she always solitary, making her lonely pilgrimages into the hills to weave her garlands, living in her private virgin's bower, and dreaming in a rather old-fashioned way – even though her proposition had sounded so aggressive, even cynical, to my non-American ears?

One Saturday evening, I was lying on my chaste hotel bed, reading, when the phone rang and I heard Rose's childish, wheedling tones. 'Professor Montague, can I come to see you?'

I was exasperated, remembering Tom Flanagan's admonition about my excessive concern for the students, and immediately regretting that I had not, for once, gone off with Gary to North Beach. 'Rose, do you realise that it is the weekend? I stayed on because I have so many papers to correct, and I certainly don't have time for student interviews. I reserve my office hours for that purpose!'

'Please,' she entreated, in the forlorn, high-pitched voice with which I was becoming wearily familiar. 'I won't stay long.'

With relief, I recalled the sign posted at the Carlton's reception desk. 'Even if I consented to see you, Rose, it wouldn't be possible. The hotel forbids "MIXED VISITORS".'

'I know. I saw that, and found it kinda funny. What do they mean by "mixed", do you think? Male or female, black or white? Racial segregation is illegal now, you know. Maybe they should take your writing course if they want to get their signs right.'

'You mean you've been to the hotel reception, and seen that notice?'

'Yeah, of course, but it doesn't apply to me,' she said lightly, with one of her gurgling laughs.

'What do you mean, it doesn't apply to you? Aren't you female, and therefore, in this context, "mixed"?' I was reflecting that she was indeed "mixed", in the sense of being mixed-up.

'It doesn't apply to me, because . . . ' – there was another suppressed giggle – 'because I've just moved into the hotel. I told you I wanted to talk to you.'

'You've moved into the hotel?' I repeated incredulously.

'That "mixed" business only applies to non-residents, visitors of guests. But now I'm a guest, just like you.' A pause. 'In fact, I got the room next door.' And to confirm this proximity, I heard a thump on my wall.

I was dry-mouthed with dread, and dismayed by what had begun to seem like the inevitability of the situation. Once more, I had been thrown up against the contrast between Rose's coy appearance – those little-girl dresses patterned with daisies above her dimpled knees – and her daring, and implacable resolve. Then there came a knock at the door.

*

My friends' reactions to the *Histoire de Rose* were various. Paule Anglim was impressed. 'She might look young,' Paule observed wryly, 'but she's a woman, not a girl. She knew what she wanted, and went after it. I'd take care, if I were you.'

Gary said, 'It's karma, man. If you're teaching the way we teach, one-on-one, and travelling with them along their spiritual path, you can't leave out the body, you know? It's part of the pilgrimage. Maybe she should hang out for a while in North Beach.'

Madeleine found the incident comically American, or, more precisely, Californian, and loyally compared my dilemma to that of the French *pompiers* (firemen), who had access to bedrooms and boudoirs at unexpected times and were notoriously *galant*. '*Il y a des politesses qu'on ne refuse pas*' was their slogan and emblem, like a modern version of the medieval knights, who would never spurn the entreaties of a lady.

Madeleine herself had come to rescue me for the Easter break, greeting old friends like the Parkinsons and the Flanagans, and generally charming everyone. Then we drove down Highway 1 again, revisiting Carmel and Robinson Jeffers' stark stone tower, which had been built to assert his Yeatsian isolation but was now part of the tourist trail. We visited Los Angeles, which reminded us of our old pal Clancy Sigal, who, years before, had directed us to a health club at Muscle Beach. (Clancy had intrigued us because, although obviously connected to Hollywood, he was no brash movie mogul, but a thin, serious young writer. Soon after that meeting in California, he would materialise at our Dublin home in another guise, as a leftist journalist and intimate of Doris Lessing.) Now Muscle Beach and

Disneyland seemed a carnivalesque version of Berkeley, and strangely soothing because less intellectually challenging.

As a member of the Comité Franc Dollar, a branch of the Patronnat, Madeleine had a professional meeting with the French consul; it seemed that there was a demand on the West Coast for mini-submarines, in which field France led the world. The consul observed that his previous post had been in Haiti, and that he did not see much difference, in either climate or mores, between Port-au-Prince and L.A. More seriously, he also hazarded some interesting comparisons between the African religious ceremonies of Haiti, and those practised in the Spanish-speaking districts of Los Angeles. We also met a famous furrier at the Beverly Hills Hotel, called Hennessy, who supplied animal pelts to the stars: he and his wife made a glittering pair.

Of course I enjoyed seeing my wife after such a protracted separation, but our affectionate banter, our knowledge of each other's habits, in fact all our familiar marital exchange, upset me as well: it was like a long-lost friend appearing abruptly, only to vanish yet again. While she was absent, the bazaar of Berkeley had been a good distraction, but her brief reappearance confused me, and after she flew back to France I felt utterly bereft.

Although every season in Berkeley was more than balmy, spring had come, with even warmer breezes, and the girls were wearing even lighter dresses in the fragrant, honeyed air. The whole campus was, as they say, 'a riot of colour'. Through Rose, I had discovered the student part of the Carlton Hotel, where the girls and boys were now sunning themselves on the roof, often topless. Hard liquor could not be served within a mile of the campus, but marijuana was as prevalent as tobacco. The whole world seemed to be, literally, going to pot, and I was not sure that I felt up to it. I wrote to Madeleine: 'I'm sorry if my last letter seemed abrupt; beginning again after Easter hasn't been easy: for a fortnight or so I really hated the Young. Living on Telegraph Avenue has its advantages, but it finally brings home to one that the indiscriminate appetite of the young applies also to oneself: your class or conversation is only one more experience to be gulped down. I will be glad to leave.'

The political ferment on campus came to a head on the twenty-first of May. I reported excitedly to Madeleine, who was ensconced in her office in a still-oblivious Paris: 'Today is Vietnam Day, a thirty-six-hour sequence of speakers, folk-singers, Norman Mailer on Lyndon Johnson, a fraternal tape from Bertrand Russell. I played my little part at 12.30 this morning when I read poems with the other Berkeley-based poets. As I write, it has already been going on for hours, and will continue all night, drums beating, speakers speaking, the campus dogs barking, all amplified on the loudspeakers and on KPFA Radio, which is relaying the whole thing. There is a real revulsion/revolution growing in the US, in which I cannot play a proper part, since I cannot feel the same pressures as them, though I do admire the whole barefoot, long-haired, banjo-sporting, guitar-plucking, love-inculcating ethos of it. An Aldermaston March generation in America might be a good thing.' I went on to describe how the East Coast was coming out to savour this new Wild West: 'Saturday and Sunday were occupied with the same disorderly circus, which climaxed with the arrival of Norman Mailer from New York.'

He was with my friend, the bohemian patroness Bananas O'Rourke, who greeted me warmly and told me that I should stay with her again at her vast apartment in the Dakota apartment building, where John Lennon would live, and die, a number of years later. I met Norman only briefly, but liked his chunky presence, like that of Dylan Thomas or Brendan Behan, those tight, round Roman men with small feet.

He made a very Maileresque speech, quoting President

Johnson as saying that he liked to have the 'peckers' of his officials in his pocket. He also described Johnson's writing style as 'the worst ever by an American president, a prose like filthy socks'. And he emphasised his various points with jabs, like a boxer, impressing the enormous stoned audience sprawled on the grass. Was it then that I heard Country Joe and the Fish, singing what had already become the anthem of the tune-in-turn-on-drop-out and anti-war movements:

> What are we fighting for?
> Don't ask me, I don't give a damn,
> Next stop is Vietnam!
> And it's five, six, seven, open up your pearly gates.
> Ain't no time to wonder why,
> Whoopee! We're all gonna die . . .

'Boys climbed the water tank on the Union [the Student Union building] to hear better, while the Cyclotron looked down in amazement from the Berkeley hills,' I wrote home to Paris.

That, for me, was the climax of the political campaign on the Berkeley campus. A second, more imaginative climax would take place when the prophets of the new American poetry gathered for an immense bardic bee, the Berkeley Poetry Conference. Charles Olsen, Robert Creeley and Allen Ginsberg were coming in from the East, and Robin Blaser, an old pal of Duncan, was planning to swoop down with his cohorts from Canada. It seemed to me the poetic equivalent of the anti-war forces amassing in the area: a call for a redefinition of poetic as well as political forces, appealing to the generous vision of Walt Whitman, as summoned by Duncan:

> It is across great scars of wrong
> I reach toward the song of kindred men
> and strike again the naked string
> old Whitman sang from.

Over my two spring semesters, I had already met many of the crucial figures in the Bay Area poetry scene. Their father figure was Kenneth Rexroth, a tough and myriad-minded little man who reminded me of Scotland's Hugh MacDiarmid, both physically and mentally: the former's tall-tale autobiography, *An Autobiographical Novel*, was nearly as garrulous and cantankerous as the latter's *Lucky Poet*. And Rexroth's intellectually sprawling Sunday-morning broadcasts on KPFA, the Bay Area's public radio station, had been a grumpy, irreverent tocsin during the moribund fifties. Both Duncan and Snyder dedicated books to Rexroth, Duncan praising 'the persistence with which you weathered out the bleak years as a sole literate person in this region . . . '. Gary praised him more privately, for being forth-rightly heterosexual in a city with such a large homosexual pop-ulation and a generally gay ethos. I also admired Rexroth, and became fascinated by his use of the seven-syllable line, especial-ly in his book-length poems. It seemed to blend philosophy and narrative in a fertile tension, like the better passages of Wordsworth's *The Prelude*: something about the cadences of Rexroth's line made his poems very readable. Years later, I would adopt and adapt this line for one of my own book-length poems, *The Dead Kingdom*.

The most notorious of the San Francisco homosexual poets was a recluse called Jack Spicer, whom Tom Parkinson's wife Ariel described to me, with a shudder, as 'a demon', though I think she meant it in the Blakean sense, since she was given to visions in her own paintings. One night in Gino & Carlo's (a lit-erary North Beach hangout like Vesuvio's, only tougher, with its rough-trade clientele gathered round the pool tables), I fell into conversation with a large, slow-moving man who looked partly American Indian. We talked about poetry, and I was very impressed by his sheer intelligence. Gary was a hive of ideas, Robert was the archetypal Blakean bard, but this man had a dry, exacting, sceptical, solitary mind. We discussed the linguistics of Benjamin Lee Whorf, the anthropology of Alfred L. Kroeber, Yeats' *A Vision*, and the complex case of noble Roger Casement.

And of course we talked about physics, which was part of the language of Berkeley, with the shadow of the Groves Project and Oppenheimer always in the background. Ironically, J. Robert Oppenheimer had also wanted to be a poet, and there was some curious affinity between the physicists and the poets: both groups were striving for a new description and definition of the universe. Charles Cattell, a fellow stammerer, was one of

Parkinson's closest friends, and had adopted me as well. And the Bevatron, which gloomed over Berkeley like a St Paul's Cathedral of science, was a fundamental particle accelerator, investigating the basic structure of matter and discovering universe within universe, the microcosm as mysterious as the macrocosm. My companion was, of course, the Jack Spicer I had been warned against. And though I never met him again, ours was the most wide-ranging and startling exchange I experienced during my time in Berkeley. He would also, with George Oppen and Charles Reznikoff, be one of the progenitors of the whole new Language Poetry movement. I commemorated the meeting in a poem, 'An Hour with Spicer':

> We only met for an hour
> Or so, before closing time
> In Gino & Carlo's
> (the clatter from the pool tables)
> And spoke of Casement's
> Knightly quest
> And how *A Vision*
> Sprang from the mind
> Of a wise woman.
>
> Squat head, fishlike
> Swollen body, you plunged
> Into the night, going
> In the opposite direction.
> Growing older,
> We speak longer and
> Longer to the dead.

Tom Parkinson and myself had been holding parties, which were a kind of prelude to the Great Poetry Conference. These took place at Tom's house, with its vast front rooms overlooking the Bay. Tom had certain edicts which had to be respected since he was the host. Jack Kerouac was never to be invited because he was 'a surly lush'; the second rule, that there was to be no hard liquor, seemed to follow from the first. On the big table in the dining room stood an array of squat jugs of rough Mountain Burgundy (Californian, of course), alongside chunks of Monterey Jack and cheddar cheese (again Californian, of course), to serve as ballast.

But in contrast to my experience of Dublin parties, everyone seemed very controlled, simply content to be in each other's company. They were nearly all there, and they were nearly all males: 'Daddy' Rexroth, Gary, Robert Duncan, Phil Whalen, Lew Welsh in his buckskins, Michael McClure and his beautiful wife – whose name, significantly, I cannot remember.

Women appeared at these gatherings nearly always as satellites to one or other of the men, and it was presumed that they would remain decoratively quiet. Gary and his pals, subtle and sensitive in so many other ways, referred to women as 'chicks' in their presence, which unnerved me, although I was used to the English and Irish term 'bird'. There were good women poets, like Gary's second wife, Joanne Kyger, who had accompanied him to Japan and India, and, of course, Duncan was working on the exfoliating vision of his H.D. book. But I remember an earlier scene at the Parkinson dining table, with the boys passing around a copy of the first *Playboy* magazine to show the female pubis. Since Joanne was present, I considered this tactless, and rebuked my pals for their adolescent gawking. It might have been, as they chortled, an advance in sexual freedom, but certainly not for women. Joanne seemed surprised but relieved by my criticism. 'No one has spoken to them like that in years,' she declared approvingly.

Allen Ginsberg, who was by now quite famous, would usually come to see Parkinson if he was in town. I lured the part-Jamaican poet Louis Simpson along a few times, and, although he subscribed more to the East Coast aesthetic and was suspicious of what Parkinson called 'the Californian branch of Glorious Poetry', he enjoyed himself as the wine flowed and he chatted to his Wild West brethren. According to Ginsberg, who had been with him at Columbia, Simpson had ignored most of the people he was now drinking with for a crucial anthology. On the other hand, those omissions had provoked the *New American Poetry* anthology of Donald Allen, a Hegelian response by the savage redskins to the sedate Eastern palefaces. That progress in poetry often seems to depend on the almost medieval disputation of schools was something I had already learnt in the fogs of Dublin, with Kavanagh trying to land a verbal knockout punch on his neo-Gaelic opponents.

A difference between the Bay Area and Dublin seemed to be that here opposites could co-exist, and the lion lie down with the lamb. (Speaking of lions, I was amused by how McClure went down to the zoo to record his poems against the background noise of their growls.) But despite the astonishing diversity of talent, which seemed almost to reflect the diversity and lushness of the local flora, I did not feel at home in California. Just as the dense hedges and parcelled fields of Ireland would always feel more familiar to me than the orange groves of California, so I responded more naturally to the poetry and politics of my home ground than to the colourful political and poetical circus in Berkeley. I knew that the great Polish poet Czeslaw Milosz cultivated his garden in Berkeley, but then his path to home was blocked by politics, while mine was opening out. My friend Roger McHugh had just become the first professor of Anglo-Irish literature at my alma mater, University College Dublin, and wanted me to come on board.

So when I went again to see that gentle scholar Henry Nash Smith, Head of Department, and he began to elaborate plans for my return to Berkeley, I had to call him to a halt.

'But I'm not coming back,' I said, to my own astonishment, while his eyes widened.

He was a courteous, soft-spoken man, an American academic gentleman of the old school, a Mark Twain scholar as well as the author of a book analysing the myth of the American West, with a title that was beginning to seem ironic, *Virgin Land.* So he did not flush and roar at me as Parkinson might have done. 'Why, may I ask, have you decided this, Professor Montague? Did the experience of working in our department displease you? I had believed that you were enjoying all the hullabaloo on our campus. We are quite prepared to raise your salary, so that you can bring Madame Montague again. She's a breath of French air!'

I found it hard to reply, since I had not been prepared for my own vehemence, had not even felt certain that I had reached a decision on this matter. But suddenly here I was, resolute, almost possessed of a vision, which I now announced. 'Of course I've enjoyed myself at Berkeley. It's probably the most pleasant university setting I will find myself in. But it's as if I had a glimpse of the Garden of Eden, and while I have revelled in it, my old-fashioned Catholic training tells me that where you have Eden there is bound to be a serpent, coiled somewhere among the eucalyptus trees.'

Professor Nash Smith looked surprised but did not contradict me. The following year, Ronald Reagan would be elected governor of California, and the Berkeley campus would be tear-gassed from the air and invaded by police and the National Guard. Right-wing America was fighting back against the Children's Crusade.

Postscript: Paradise Lost

Of course I soon regretted my decision, announced in such dramatic and irrevocable terms, and had many doubts and gloomy afterthoughts. Had I broken off the possibility of an academic career in America, something I had thought I did not covet but which I might, after all, long for in the years to come? Perhaps they would pass on the word that I was not sufficiently grateful for their confidence in me, despite my (I had to admit) rather modest credentials, an Irish MA and only two slim volumes of poetry and a fatter book of short stories to my name. Of course this situation would soon change, when writing workshops began to flourish across the colleges, and teachers were taken on not because of their academic prowess but simply because they were published creative writers. Indeed, the poet Thom Gunn would be able to give up full-time teaching in the once rigidly formal Berkeley and negotiate a much more flexible contract. But in 1965 there was still only the one portal through which one might enter the university, and Berkeley had been particularly kind to me in that regard.

There were many rites of farewell to be accomplished, which kept me busy. My San Francisco poet pals arranged a reading to celebrate my forthcoming book, *A Chosen Light*, some of which had been written on the campus. It included 'All Legendary Obstacles', a poem of love and yearning for Madeleine, set in the former railway station at Berkeley, which had taken me a decade to get right. The San Francisco poets were gratifyingly enthusiastic, especially considering the formal nature of my poems. But these American poets thought the book widened the arc of Irish poetry to embrace international themes – love poems as well as poems about the bog.

I found myself in a kind of poetic halfway house between California and the East. Gary and myself had a friendly farewell discussion about the long poems we were respectively working on, and which were supposed to sum up our separate cultures.

'How do you see the shape of your monster?' I asked him as we were placidly drinking wine in his compact apartment. (He had long ago despaired of teaching me the lotus position. I had come close to achieving it, but my Irish legs would invariably begin to ache after a while, whereas Gary, it seemed, could fold up like a deckchair and sustain the position all evening long.)

He opened his arms wide. 'I see it like a Japanese or Chinese scroll, something opening out on either side, with mountains and mists and seas, and small figures moving against that background. A kind of glimpse of infinity. In fact, I'm calling it *Mountains and Rivers Without End*.'

'Well, I can't comment on the quality of a work I haven't seen. But there's one thing certain. Mine will be finished before yours. Infinite mountains and seas are one thing, but mine will be called *The Rough Field*, which has hedges and can be ploughed.'

Sure enough, Gary sent the first cantos of *Mountains and Rivers Without End* to me in Paris. The complete poem would not appear until several decades later, however, long after the vogue for that particular kind of long poem, in open form, seemed to have passed – which did not diminish its beauty, splendour and energy, as lovely as the best of Pound's *Cantos*.

Before I left, I took to spending weekends at Paule Anglim's place, doing the rounds of the art galleries. The San Francisco Museum had a fair selection from the West Coast art movement, from Mark Tobey to Richard Diebenkorn, and a lovely painting of a wounded bird by my friend Morris Graves. But what astonished and delighted me most was the first big exhibition of Indian art, housed, ironically, in the Palace of the Legion of Honor, a solemnly opulent structure which evoked for me the larger rooms of Madeleine's family seat in Normandy.

Some of the great erotic sculptures, which created a sensation when featured in the *Evergreen Review*, published by Barney Rosset and the Grove Press, were there, from Shiva and Parvati, equally balanced in the ecstasy of their dance, to the temple frescoes with their interlacing bodies. I sent postcards of these lush, noble goddesses back to the Rue Daguerre, to prepare for my homecoming. All my exposure to the Berkeley style of consciousness-raising, with its combination of wholesomeness and abandon, had not moved me half as much as did these exquisite figures, which seemed at once passionate and serene. Finally, I believed I could accept Gary's tantric ideal of releasing the spiritual through the physical, because this exhibition had let me see how lovemaking could have a religious aspect, the achievement of *mithuna*, a mutual celebration of the divine creative energy. The erotic experiments of 1960s Berkeley seemed naive and awkward in comparison with these smiling, ancient figures.

Afterwards I walked for hours in Golden Gate Park, admiring the grazing buffalo, clambering along the cliffs above the great Pacific. I seemed to have found what I had come for, a precious cargo I could carry home. Although perhaps I should have stayed for the aforementioned great Berkeley Poetic Potlatch, and confirmed my place among them, in the manner of Denise Levertov, an English-Welsh-Jewish woman who had become part of that poetic community. Certainly there was an affinity between myself and my San Francisco confrères, and whenever we met in years to come, at poetry festivals across the world, the old Californian cameraderie would warm us again. I read with Ginsberg in Rotterdam and with McClure in Amsterdam, and accompanied Duncan through a swift visit to Paris, as though he had swooped in on a broomstick. Later, Denise Levertov and Bob Creeley would stay in my Cork home.

One way or another, my link with California never seemed to break. In fact, just a few years ago, a little while before Allen died, my wife Elizabeth and I were visiting downtown New York. One evening we noticed that a photography gallery on leafy Washington Square was announcing an exhibition of Beat poets, due to open the following day. But for some reason the door was open, so we ventured tentatively into the airy space. And there they were, examining large, flamboyant photographs of themselves, Allen, Mike McClure and Ted Joans. 'Hi, John,' cried Mike jauntily, as if we'd parted only yesterday. Allen, looking much frailer and older, but with the same burning, intelligent gaze, gave me a resounding kiss on the mouth and greeted Elizabeth affectionately. Then Ted and I had a long chat about old friends. But what struck me was that not one of them seemed surprised to see me there, as if our connection was as warm and immediate as ever. So perhaps I need not have been so wistful when I had left California in the mid-sixties.

But after my successful terms there, when they wanted another Irish poet to spend a full year on the campus, I recommended a young man called Seamus Heaney, who was growing more and more uneasy in turbulent Belfast. I hoped that he would be well able to adapt to the luxuriant landscape and stimulating atmosphere of Berkeley. And since his wife Marie would accompany him, I knew that he would not be in danger of succumbing to the loneliness that I had struggled with in that beautiful but various place. Perhaps the serpent that I had predicted lay sleeping in the garden would not awake too soon.

PART II

2

Paris Interlude

Despite the political upheavals in America, which seemed to justify my decision, I continued to ask myself why I did not stay on in Berkeley. I suppose the answer is that I was neither a young American nor a traditional Frenchman accustomed to erotic adventures, but still (as Gary Snyder shrewdly discerned) to some degree an old-fashioned Ulster Catholic.

So my decision to leave Berkeley was largely due to a desire for moorings, and for a marital intimacy that both myself and Madeleine had neglected. These days, when husband and wife both may have jobs, long-distance marriages have become par for the course. But in the mid-1960s, Madeleine and I had few models for our unconventional arrangement, and the long separations were damaging the foundations of our mutual trust. So, after I renounced Berkeley, more or less permanently (Adam expelling himself from the garden, or Ulysses evading Circe?), I sought another solution, back home in Europe.

*

Paris was still wonderful, of course, but I felt almost too pampered there, with my few hours of creative work in the morning, after Madeleine had left for her office, and the long indolent afternoons to explore the city. My job as Paris correspondent for the *Irish Times* had been interrupted by my absence in California.

Now that the Algerian war appeared to have been resolved, I had less interest anyway, although the CRS, or riot police, were still in evidence in the streets – a presence disturbing to someone of my fraught Ulster background; I felt that they were spoiling to use those sinister billy clubs again, as indeed they soon would.

Reviewing, even for *Le Monde* and the *Guardian*, did not amount to a living wage, and the additional poetic tasks I had saddled myself with, including campaigning for the neglected poetry of John Hewitt, and collecting the erratic Kavanagh, were not enough to keep me decently busy. Of course there was my long poem *The Rough Field*, sections of which I was beginning to publish, as well as another marvellous long-term project, *The Faber Book of Irish Verse*, which would require an extensive rethinking of the whole Irish poetic tradition and would take a Herculean seven years to complete.

This task had been passed on to me by my diplomat poet pal Val Iremonger. Grappling with an incipient breakdown, and seeking relief from the Court of St James, he found himself transferred to what he called 'the ant's arsehole' of Stockholm, during the coldest winter Sweden had experienced in years. He was so disenchanted by his new post, he took to watching Ingmar Bergman's gloomiest films obsessively, and, when he met Bergman himself, declared that the director was 'the most cheerful man in Sweden'.

Not Driving, But Swearing

These labours of love were drawing out the best in me, yet neither required my presence in Paris, except in the sense of distance bringing greater objectivity. Nevertheless, I continued my efforts to put down frail roots in French society. One was learning to drive, and I launched into a series of lessons in the Auto-École Daguerre. Figure Madeleine's surprise when I passed first time, changing gears with scarcely a screech, parking adroitly, and remaining unruffled by the choleric French drivers waving their arms at one another and exchanging ritual insults: '*Espèce de con! Enculé! Putain de merde!*'

There was only one small hitch: I baulked at the orals, which were, of course, in French. It was that old nemesis, my stammer, with my brain refusing to comprehend the rapid-fire French signals, which I actually knew quite well. No matter, this would be easy to rectify, and when I came home from Berkeley, I hastened to pass my orals. I breezed through them, in fact, and now felt that I was a fully qualified French driver. But the inspector was a certain kind of officious civil servant: small, scowling, determined to exercise his authority, a bureaucratic Napoleon. Assuming that I was English, he grilled and grilled me, clearly disappointed that I did not, this time, stumble.

But finally he found the opening he wanted. I might have passed my orals but, as he frowned over my dossier, he announced triumphantly, 'It has been more than a year since you passed your driving test. We'd better see how you are behind the wheel before we turn you loose on Paris.' Smirking, he led me to the car used for testing, while I tried to conceal my indignation behind a serene smile. Inwardly, however, recalling the lively insults I'd learnt from French drivers, I seethed, 'Listen, you *fils de pute*, you *salopard*, I'll show you how I can drive!'

We glided into the Paris evening traffic, a steel-sheathed stream. Briskly, I dealt with traffic lights, accelerated down long avenues, swung cautiously around corners. Not a word from my stiff companion, neither critical nor admiring. Then came a crossing where lights were on the point of changing. 'Stop,' he said at last.

'No,' I replied, determined to demonstrate my knowledge of Paris, 'we have enough time.' And I shot over the intersection before yellow dissolved into red.

'That's enough!' he cried. 'I do not want to die for England! You drive too quickly for someone who is not French. You will have to pass your driving test again.'

It seemed I could not convince this tiny martinet that I was not an Anglo-Saxon. Perhaps I should have echoed Beckett, who, when asked was he English, replied, '*Au contraire.*' But in addition to being hubristic about my driving prowess, I did not have the good sense to humour my autocratic instructor by playing the usual Irish card. I think I was too fascinated by his naked dislike for '*Perfide Albion*' to challenge him.

It was all downhill from then on. Having passed the orals, I began failing the practical. Twice more, and the man who had passed his first French, indeed Parisian, driving test with flying colours had become a nervous Nellie, depending on other drivers, usually Madeleine.

The one thing I had acquired from my driving days was the rhetoric of ceremonial insult which was, and still is, so important in France. In fact, it was from this kind of artillery fire that some of Beckett's best dramatic scenes spring. A typical exchange could begin simply enough. If someone made a wrong turn, or bumped into your car, you could call them '*Tête de noeud*', or

'Noodle head'. Or you could snarl at an elderly person '*Vieux chameau*' ('Old camel') – hardly courteous. More imaginatively, there is '*Vieux chalumeau oxydé*' ('Shrivelled-up old marsh-mallow').

Women drivers were often targeted, obviously with '*Conasse*', but more distinctly with '*Petasse*' or '*Pouffiasse*'. If the woman was large and awkward, she would invariably be '*Une grosse vache*'. Men, on the other hand, were more dangerous, especially if they were larger and stronger than oneself. '*Conard*' is the masculine equivalent of '*Conasse*' – a scathing insult, though an anatomical impossibility. '*Enculé*', or 'Bugger', raised the stakes, especially '*Espèce d'enculé*'. But the real drama came when you moved to aspersions on the other driver's family. '*Et ta soeur*' was growled while wheeling down the window. (Although, unlike in Spain and Italy, '*Ta mère*' was seldom used: something was sacred in these stylised diatribes.) The other driver was then meant to open his door just a fraction and ask, with dangerous mildness, '*Et comment?*' at which point it would be prudent to press on the accelerator. After all, people have had heart attacks in French car parks.

This was to say nothing of old people trudging across the road. Madeleine's slight, distinguished boss at the Patronnat (the highly conservative employers' union, or 'Boss Brigade') would cruise through the French countryside on a Sunday, gliding along the leafy roads and through villages at high speed. Young and old alike were scattered like petals from his path, but he especially enjoyed making old ladies scuttle to safety, crying out the window: '*Hoop la, grandmère!*'

I was quite amused to learn the absolute worst of these ceremonial vehicular insults. No, it was nothing to do with the driver's parentage or progeny. No, it did not scourge him or her in terms of looks, character or intelligence. The most scathing, the most unendurable, insult one could muster was '*Banlieusard*', or 'Suburbanite'.

Expatriate Life

We also tried to resume the same pattern of casual hospitality we had established in Dublin's Herbert Street, with dinner parties, and parties *tout simple*, restricted by the almost doll's-house size of the studio. Madeleine still had some bohemian friends from her days working in a bookshop in the Rue de Seine, and our little band of Irish expatriates, like Con Leventhal and Peter Lennon, would sometimes ring our rustic doorbell. And then there was the growing number of my French poet friends, who were not really party animals in the Anglo-Saxon sense but were usually glad to see each other. Our painter friends would also drop by. (In my experience, painters are always glad of a party, and have a flair for throwing them.)

And to my first birthday party in Paris came that plucky lady Sylvia Beach, with her piping voice and halo of white hair. She had a bottle of champagne under her oxter, and had brought a torch to guide her up the cobblestones of our little courtyard, having spurned the offer of a lift, even though she was well over seventy, and as frail as a figurine. Sylvia had recently become involved in the creation of the Joyce Museum at the Martello Tower in Sandycove, which had been bought by our architect friend Michael Scott long before. He had daringly designed his own modern house on the property but had later decided that this literary and historical monument should be revived as a national treasure, with a museum to celebrate those famous opening pages of *Ulysses*, a book which, of course, Sylvia had been the first to publish.

And that same year, 1966, in another attempt to re-create the halcyon days of expatriate exuberance, there was a big poetry reading at the American Center in the Boulevard Raspail, organised by Patrick Bowles, who had worked with Beckett on the English version of *Molloy*, and Leonard Radlo, director of the centre. We did not revive the spirit of the 1920s, when Hemingway had boxed there, but there was a full and enthusiastic house. Maria Jolas, widow of Eugene, the editor of *Transition*, came along, a sturdy Kentucky lady with a strong sense of humour and a robust singing voice. Her daughter, Betsy, was a distinguished composer, trying to hold her own in a man's world: as far as I know, she was the first woman to write an opera. From visiting Sylvia in the Rue de l'Odéon, and Maria in the Rue de Rennes, I had some sense of the milieu in which Joyce had moved, supported and surrounded by these brave women.

A possible connection with my Californian days was when Allen Ginsberg and his partner Peter Orlovsky, along with others of their wild coterie, landed up in a small hotel in the Rue Git le Coeur, where they practised a systematic *derèglement de tous les sens*, according to the prescription of Rimbaud. But I did not feel like joining them; while I was at ease with my homosexual friends, of course I was not *of* them. William S. Burroughs arrived, probably from Tangier, and I met him with Allen in an English-language bookshop in the Rue de Seine. I found Burroughs even more laconic than Beckett, a cadaverous, ashen-faced man whose old-fashioned, solemn courtesy reminded me of that of an undertaker, or of my gloomy uncle-in-law Henry, who could always manage to dampen any conversation. Part of Burroughs' lurid trilogy, *Naked Lunch*, had appeared from the Olympia Press in 1962, but I was not into sexual science fiction, nor really into drugs. I had of course flirted with pot and hash in Berkeley, but the darker world of needles scared me.

The more sedate *Paris Review* had an office in a street near the Odéon, but I did not often drop in. American literature was in the ascendant, but in many ways the American ex-pats struck me as provincial. For them, the American reality was pervasive. Even when they walked along the avenues of the rive gauche, or entered a café, the atmosphere would sometimes change, as if their loud cheerful voices, their poor or non-existent French, and their hearty style of greeting and drinking crowded out everything around them.

The novelist James Jones had a fine apartment on the Île de St Louis, Ezra Pound's image of urban serenity in *The Pisan Cantos*. James told me, over a drink in the Coupole, that he had been back to the States, and that the people he met there, in the country clubs of all places, were 'the salt of the earth'. 'I don't see why people criticise them,' he exclaimed. 'They're some of the finest people you'd ever meet.'

Most of the American writers then living in Paris seemed only to have restaurant French, unlike James Baldwin and Herbert Gold in the early fifties. A writer I ought to have got to know was the brilliantly fluent John Ashbery, who was the art critic for the *International Herald Tribune*. But although I already knew some of the staff writers there, including Charlie Monaghan and Jim Brown, old-school gourmets and guzzlers both, I never happened to meet the author of *The Tennis Court Oath*.

The Reluctant Englishman and The Wild Irish Girl

But the most important meeting in Paris for me was with Desiree Moorehead and Bill Hayter, at a party given by Darthea Speyer, who was yet another well-known American patron of the arts, and ran a fine gallery in the Latin Quarter. Desiree was vibrant and vivacious, with a throaty laugh, immense blue eyes and profuse hair, a genuine Irish beauty, while Bill, a first-class engraver and serious painter, was a lean, wiry Englishman many years her senior. The dynamic between them was intense: they had met only recently, yet he was determined to rescue this confident though guileless girl from the wilder shores of bohemia. I accompanied them to a concert of Elizabethan music, only to have the delicate tones of Alfred Deller punctuated by a hissing exchange between the pair, with myself acting as referee and peacemaker.

I liked Desiree not only for her vitality, but because it struck me that she was the latest in a long line of high-spirited Irish girls who had set out to conquer France. La Belle O'Morphee is celebrated in François Boucher's rosy erotic paintings; Johanna Heffernan, with her abundant auburn hair, was Gustave Courbet's mistress and muse; Harriet Smithson haunted Berlioz. And now there was Desiree Moorehead, from a Dublin family, cutting a swath through Paris.

Desiree and Bill always lived together in and around his large studio, where the paintings and engravings accumulated. He also had a famous workshop, Atelier 17, which he had founded in 1927 and which is still going strong. According to Beckett's

oldest Irish friend, Con Leventhal, Bill's workshop was, as a cat-
alogue of an exhibition in Dublin arranged by Bruce Arnold put
it, 'a kind of commune in which each member is free to pursue
his own impulse, and at the same time discuss with and seek
advice of his fellow artists. Some idea of its attraction may be
given by considering that such well-known figures, for example,
as [Joan] Miró, [Yves] Tanguy and [Hans] Arp worked happily
and constructively with lesser lights in the firmament of this
informal studio.' Madeleine was impressed by the brisk, physical
aspects of engraving, and watched Bill scour a plate with a page
from an old *Le Monde* and then bend over it with the burin, or
chisel. Bill's students came from everywhere – Japan and India
as well as Europe – and while he taught them the techniques he
describes in his classic *New Ways of Gravure*, they were encouraged to develop their own vision. They formed a diverse, lively,
chattering group in the cafés near the Rue Daguerre, and sometimes at parties in the studio. When they left, they would become
filaments in the living web of Bill's former students around the
world.

Evenings chez Hayter were wonderful, as we lingered long
over the aperitifs in a space surrounded by books and prints. Bill
had been trained as a scientist, with degrees in chemisty and
geology from King's College London, and his comprehension of
how the world works created a fertile tension between science
and art that has seldom been attained since the Renaissance and
Leonardo's notebooks. To hear him talk of ecology, or theories
of cosmology, was to listen like the wedding guest, entranced: he
always spoke with the same swiftness and intensity, making one
a companion in the search.

The conversation continued, uninterrupted, at the table.
Madeleine was intrigued that Hayter paid slight attention to the
social structure of France, being far more interested in the
artists who had flourished there. Her family and colleagues

conducted a different kind of social exchange, peppered with *mondanités*. She would pretend to be surprised when, at the end of the evening, Bill and I would box, in a light-hearted version of Hemingway at the American Center. I had a long reach, and could move swiftly, while Bill was smaller. But he was hawkish in attack, seizing every chance to clip me on the ear. Desiree was supposed to be timekeeper, but she usually got absorbed in the drama, like Scott Fitzgerald with Hemingway, and forgot to call time. Later, especially if she was flushed with just the right amount of drink, she would dance – a wild, abandoned dance of her own, like Isadora Duncan or a veiled Salome, or like James Joyce's ritual dance before the guests went home.

I suppose that our own casual gatherings at the Rue Daguerre, as well as those sprawling, stimulating Hayter evenings, were at variance with certain French ideas about how to conduct a social life. The writers and painters whom we knew, and who enjoyed our kind of exuberant party-throwing, were a bohemian minority. Most French people would feel obliged to sustain an urbane – and sometimes dull – style of exchange at parties, being too *bien élevé* to raise disturbing subjects. Table manners were also invariably an issue: if one dared to eat a peach, its skin should be unfurled neatly with knife and fork. So Bill's uncompromising intellectualism, his disdain for bourgeois values, his ability to make dazzling connections between art and science as if drawing strands out of the air, were more unconventional than I realised, like Desiree's coltish vivacity. In short, this was not how one was supposed to behave in good society.

Madeleine's elder brother was an architect, but her family in general seemed to have little or no interest in the arts, nor did they appear to know any artists or writers apart from me, an exotic Irish import. They were, in fact, something like the peers of England, passionate about horses and hunting, tenderly involved with family, and largely indifferent to sedentary pursuits. During those genteel weekends at Bellozane in the Normandy countryside, neither art nor politics was discussed, just family matters. The only comment concerning poetry, offered by her younger brother, was when he asked me, with polite incredulity, '*Comment va les petits poèmes?*' (And her distinguished boss at the Patronnat, after routinely inquiring as to my occupation and being told that I wrote poetry, exclaimed, '*Ça ce fait encore!*') In light of all this, I appreciated Madeleine's generally amused acceptance of, and indeed involvement with, the bohemian world of writers and artists. Despite, or perhaps because of, her conservative background, she was nearly always eager for lively experiences; it seemed part of her intrepid nature.

And she was not without party pieces of her own. For a strong, fairly tall woman, Madeleine had a surprisingly high-pitched, piping voice; in fact, one of my pet names for her was 'Squeaky'. And when she raised that light voice in song, it was plangent and sweet, especially when she sang the medieval French songs that she loved. Many French songs have an appealing, childlike sweetness, and Madeleine's favourites were especially whimsical, like '*Mon Père M'a Donné Un Mari*', about a father who gives his daughter a tiny husband: '*Mon père m'a donne un mari,/ Mon Dieu, quel homme, quel petit homme!*' The 'little husband' almost comes to a bad end, first getting lost in his bride's vast bed, then being scorched by her candle as she's searching for him, then nearly being gobbled up by the cat, who mistakes him for a mouse. 'Don't eat him!' the bride implores her cat. 'He's so small!' Madeleine also sang a more tender, romantic song, which was cherished by Robert Graves – and which, indeed, he quotes in full in *The White Goddess*. This song, called '*Aux Marches du Palais*', contains some of those strange, dreamlike images particular to medieval times. A princess chooses, from her many suitors, a little cobbler. They sleep together in a large bed through which a deep river flows, and they will lie there, together, until the end of time. Everyone loved hearing her sing these two ancient songs, though it did strike me as curious that in both of them there is a small man and an enormous bed!

Hayter's association with Irish writers had begun in the thirties, with his *Work-in-Progress* (1936), a title borrowed from the serialisation of *Finnegans Wake* in *Transition*. Round about the same time, Hayter was associated with the surrealists; he had exhibited in the first surrealist exhibition in London, in 1936. George Reavey, that strange little linen merchant's son from the north of Ireland, had drafted Bill to illustrate a cover for his own *Nostradam*, and an early book of poems by Brian Coffey, *Third Person*, both published by Reavey's Europa Press. So it was natural that he and I should collaborate. Bill executed a suite of six etchings of the sea, very delicate yet dense, with undulating lines, for which I tried to find a verbal equivalent. After looking long at those great sweeps of colour and enmeshed lines, I produced my sequence, 'Sea Changes', which would appear as the last section of *Tides*:

> For there is no sea
> it is all a dream
> there is no sea
> except in the tangle
> of our minds:
> the wine dark
> sea of history
> on which we all turn
> turn and thresh
> and disappear.

It would be hard for me to do justice to the effect Bill Hayter had on my own imagination. I learnt from him how to see the world as a complex of energies, a dance of chance and necessity. He was always fascinated by wind and wave, down to the minutest detail, busily explaining, for example, how a stone in a pool creates 'a standing wave', something that fishing had also taught the Yeats who wrote 'Easter, 1916'. And perhaps because engraving is a briskly physical art, he, as workmanlike as Blake, did not lose himself in the coarse commercialism that had begun to transform works of art into merchandise, when, as Robert Graves says, 'the architects have sold the pass, and will destroy to further their kind of cold expensive beauty'. Hayter, artist and teacher, always worked with, not against, the forces of life.

An amusing coda: an intense friendship between an Englishman and an Irishman often is, I find, a mixture of sweetness and sharpness, as our national traits collide or collude. For example, Bill loved Elizabethan music, as I did myself, especially because of its link with the lyric poetry which had flowered at that time; one of our finer minor poets, Thomas MacDonagh, executed in 1916, had made a study of Campion. MacDonagh had also investigated, in his book *Literature in Ireland*, the relationship between the rhythms of Irish music and poetry. And partly under that influence, Claddagh Records was producing renderings of some of the oldest Irish songs, the often harsh plangency of *sean nos*. But Bill would have none of this: it grated upon his sensibility, like the scringe of chalk upon a slate in the schoolroom, or like our collie dog at home in Garvaghey, who, when Aunt Freda played the piano, would raise his noble nose and howl derisively. Groaning at the nasal twangs and quaverings of *sean nos*, or the elisions in the fiddle playing of a master like Denis Murphy, Bill would cry, 'But they can't even carry a tune!' As these were often masterpieces of an older art form, which we had patiently recovered, I would explain to him, in a long-suffering way, the subtlety of the notes, the equivalent of assonance in Old Irish poetry. If I could listen to the simperings of his English eunuchs, who sounded like the castrati of medieval choirs, why would he not make the same allowance for an even older art?

'Never!' Bill bristled like a bulldog whose fur had been stroked the wrong way, and bared his teeth at this Hibernian cacophony. (Actually Samuel Beckett, although he had let his work be recorded by Claddagh, did not like the native Irish sound much either – classically trained as he was. And he loathed that hallowed Irish habit, the dreaded sing-song. His detestation of someone suddenly breaking into caterwauling melodies, as he viewed it, in public extended even to Maria Jolas, whom he liked – although not her tendency to raise her strong Kentucky voice spontaneously in song.)

Almost a Star

I had studiously avoided meeting Sartre, although sometimes I found myself in that then louche late-night bar, the Falstaff, with Beckett at the same time as Jean-Paul, spectacles glinting while he attacked his *steak frites*. We would exchange the Parisian equivalent of the West Cork 'farmer's nod' between neighbours but did not speak. But then I got drawn into a project for filming his long story about the Spanish Civil War, '*Le Mur*' ('The Wall'), with an intense young French director, Serge Roullet. Serge had a weakness for casting writers instead of professional actors. He had a theory that they would show more genuine emotion, and also suspected that this way of working would please Jean-Paul. Serge had already chosen a distinguished expatriate novelist, Michel del Castillo, for one lead part, and wanted me to try for the other, saying, '"Montague" sounds well, and you have a fine English *profil*.' Having been a film critic for years, I was flattered, despite the unintended slight on my good Hibernian head.

So I spent days in a desolate barn in the outskirts of Paris, repeating the same phrase again and again as the cameras glided and whirred around me. Visually speaking, it seemed that I was a triumph – as photogenic as any fledgling star. But nothing could disguise my stammer, which was usually only barely noticeable in French, since it sounded like a foreigner's natural hesitation as he searches for *le mot juste*. When one is trying to make a film, an interminable process at the best of times, a stammer doubles the number of takes required. The crew were astounded at first, because generally the French don't stammer; they presumed that mine was a pleasantly eccentric English affectation. But as I glooped and gargled, all the more so because of the glaring lights and febrile atmosphere of a film set, they began to exchange glances, fearing that the whole project would be gobbled up by my glottal stops. '*Ils ont tirait un bon moment*' ('They fired for a good while') I creaked again and again, until Serge finally threw in the towel.

He would not give up my noble head, however, and conscripted me in a minor role, as the English-speaking prisoner from the international brigade, chatting to his mate in prison – the closest I would ever get to Orwell and Hemingway. My fellow prisoner was a sweet young gay Protestant man from the north of Ireland, who had taken over my lead part of 'Tom'. Our brief prison meeting caused us much wry mirth, since we were meant to be Englishmen but were actually, of course, two Northern Irishmen, one Catholic, the other Protestant, at a time when the Ulster problem was just beginning to rear its ugly head again. My poet neighbour Claude Esteban was also drafted in for a brief appearance, as a character called Pablo, and we exchange salutations towards the end of the film. '*Pablo, sacré veinard!*' ('Pablo, you blessed scoundrel!') became our ritual greeting.

Sartre and Simone de Beauvoir came to the film's opening, early in 1967, but although the production had one of the best literary casts in recent history – a novelist and two poets (Michel del Castillo, Claude and myself) – it sank almost without a ripple. Serge was full of plans to produce another highly literary film, on a Melville story, but I refused to be drafted this time, recognising that my career as a movie star was, alas, over. Our little film, however, had considerable success throughout South America, and I have occasionally found myself being greeted enthusiastically by some Latin American film buff as if I were a revolutionary hero like Che Guevera. Indeed, my 'English head' appears in one of the publicity stills used to promote the film in that part of the world.

71

Many moons later, I met some of the minor figures involved in the making of *Le Mur*. I was back in Paris for a *soirée littéraire* at the Centre Pompidou, trying to reassemble the facets of my French literary life for this 'Montague presentation'. I was lucky enough, since several of my translators were in town, distinguished poets like Michel Deguy and Esteban. The poet and alchemist Robert Marteau was too aloof to read, but the ebullient Gaston Miron had blown in from Montreal, and read for Marteau, interspersing his recital with blasts from his mouth organ. Part of the poetic population of Paris was there, and, of course, many Irish exiles and ex-pats, pleased to hear the poetry as well as the Irish music that opened the programme. The enthusiastic crowd even managed to laugh when the then literary director, who had not drawn a sober breath all week, brought the evening to a surprising close by thanking '*l'ambassadeur d'Iceland*' – whereupon the Irish ambassador rose and bowed stylishly, without breaking diplomatic decorum beyond giving a rueful grin. (This reminds me of a diplomatic crisis of my own, involving the mispronunciation of a name. When the lofty English poet Stephen Spender read after me at Benjamin Britten's Aldeburgh Festival in the 1980s, he graciously thanked the Irish poet 'John Montgomery' for his entertaining verses. What could I do but take a leaf from the Irish ambassador's book, and bow serenely?)

Desiree organised a splendid post-reading party in the Rue Cassini. The rotund Breton poet Eugene Guillevic was there, and we had a half-amused, half-serious exchange about 'Celtitude'. He had been born and reared in Carnac, with its mysterious menhirs, about which he had written a long poem that I would later translate. André Frenaud had, I think, overcome his usual reluctance to attend an English-speaking gathering. Among the readers and revellers was a well-known young French actor, Pierre Clementi, the sombre, smouldering bad guy of *Belle de Jour*, with whom I had read 'Hymn to the New Omagh Road' in tandem. We discussed that eternal problem, whether poetry is better served when read by the poet or by an actor. To illustrate his preference, he mounted some steps and growled a few lines from Baudelaire.

Desiree was everywhere, replenishing glasses, and laughing and talking with everyone. If Paris had always welcomed my poetry as warmly as that, I would have had no reason to leave it.

3

DUBLIN REVISITED

PREFACE: DUBLIN FROM A HEIGHT

Failed film star, failed driver, I looked about me for further projects beyond the Faber anthology and my own unfurling long poem, but Paris was yielding little except for the occasional unpaid publication for people like Maurice Nadeau, in his high-brow *Quinzaine Littéraire* and *Les Lettres Nouvelles*. Again, Roger McHugh came to my rescue, suggesting that I should join his new Anglo-Irish Department, which had burgeoned from his early extra-mural lectures on the Irish Literary Revival at University College Dublin. As a student, I had attended those lectures, which were my first glimpse into our early-twentieth-century literature, and Roger was now repaying my interest. So after a year or so at home in Paris, in the early spring of 1967 I found myself back in gloomy, rainy Georgian Dublin, one of my favourite backdrops:

> A quiet evening, with skies washed and grey;
> A tiredness as though the day
> Swayed towards sleep,
> Except for the reserved statement
> Of rain on the stone-grey pavement . . .

I rented a large, old-fashioned flat at the top of a quayside house in Anglesea Street in what is now Temple Bar. It was a legendary place: Brendan Behan, a young painter called Roger Shackleton, and many other artistic refugees had lived there. The skylight above my typewriter reminded me of the Rue Daguerre, and on the big table in the main room I laid out my books and my tarot pack; I was teaching a seminar on the early Yeats, and studying the Mysteries. It was a short stroll up to the old UCD in Earlsfort Terrace, where I gave seminars in an upper room for Roger, and lectured in large halls for my contemporary, Denis Donoghue, now professor of Modern English and American Literature. The contrast between my small graduate seminar, with eager, intelligent young Americans like Thomas Dillon Redshaw, and the mass of students thronging the lecture hall like cattle, foreshadowed the move of UCD from the city centre to the prairies of Belfield.

If I wanted to be on my own, I would cross the Liffey over the Ha'penny Bridge to buy paraffin for my oil heater, or to see a lonely film in bustling, tawdry O'Connell Street. If I sought companionship, I would shoot up to Grafton Street to have lunch in Neary's or the Bailey, which had been bought by the former editor of *Envoy*, John Ryan, now a genial host presiding over the literary and political turmoil of 'Graftonia'. Kavanagh might be there with his future wife, Katherine Moloney; or that fine novelist Gerry Hanley, who had been one of the first writers to deal with the theme of the Empire in decline; or Liam O'Flaherty, ice-blue eyes smiling or scowling as the mood took him. Liam was as unpredictable as the seas of his native Aran: after one set-to, he informed me that he had been enquiring in France as to how much it would cost to get rid of me, but had decided, 'Montague, you're not worth the expense.' Such talk, even idly expressed, chilled me, but for Liam it was the height of humour.

Yet a minor shift in artistic sensibility had occurred in Dublin since Kavanagh's infamous libel action against the *Leader* magazine. McDaids, the bohemian shark tank of a decade, had begun to lose its introverted, sour attraction, and when its brilliant chief barman, Paddy O'Brien, died, and a new owner came in, the whole atmosphere changed. The sharp-tongued literary lot gradually moved on to Grogan's, causing me to coin a bon mot, which, like a joke or an anonymous lyric, was soon absorbed into the local folk memory. But believe it or not, it was I who first declared of the denizens of McDaids and their exile from their old watering hole: 'This must be the first time in history that the sinking ship deserted the rats.'

I was trying to settle back into the Dublin that we had left half a decade before, hoping that Madeleine and I could gather up the unravelling threads of our previous life together. We had always tried to keep up our old connections, and there was one marvellous summer when we had stayed for a few weeks at our former home in Herbert Street while our erstwhile landlord-and-lady, the Doyle-Kellys, were away. We gave a party in the back garden, which was almost like old times. Paddy Moloney tootled his whistle, Ben Kiely told a story in his deep honeyed voice, Tom Kinsella sang a parody of a folk song which had been a favourite of Brendan Behan, and we all lofted our glasses in the evening sunlight, until a stray northerner from Omagh sparked a quarrel.

But while the cast of characters seemed similar, there were telling changes. Kavanagh was still around, but was clearly not well, coughing and spluttering like an old tractor engine in the corner of a pub, or sighing to himself 'Oh dear, oh dear', but with a darker intonation than the White Rabbit! His *Collected Poems* had appeared in 1964 to some acclaim, and a dramatisation of *Tarry Flynn* was in prospect for the Abbey. So he was content enough in literary terms, although his few new poems seemed to scrape the barrel of the self. He would die a few months later, in 1967, at the relatively young age of sixty-three, his robust rural constitution finally broken down by years of disappointment and poverty, and attendant heavy drinking.

Our other senior poet, Austin Clarke, was sailing beyond seventy, better humoured because better known, due to the efforts of Liam Miller and his Dolmen Press. After *Later Poems* came *Flight to Africa*, a lengthy and lively book for a man who had just survived two heart attacks. Our battle campaign to celebrate the natural terracing of generations in Irish poetry seemed to be working, with Kavanagh and Clarke as senior figures, and Kinsella, Richard Murphy and myself trotting along afterwards. I can now see that my desire to reinvent or champion my elders was born of more than a literary impulse, being connected with my thwarted need to rescue my own broken family tree. If I could do little for the father I had barely known, I could at least try to help my *poetic* fathers.

The distress of such noble yet neglected figures as Kavanagh and Clarke touched me deeply. Still awash with youthful energy, I sought every chance to assist them, and to restore a normal literary life of the kind I had glimpsed in Paris. One of my first sights of Kavanagh was at the UCD reading of Robert Frost, who was sweeping through Europe on a triumphal tour. Kavanagh sprawled on one of the front benches of the Physics Theatre, looking haggard and ill. The contrast between the silver-haired, Horatian, gentleman-farmer poet and the crumpled figure of Kavanagh, who, unlike Frost, had actually been born and bred on a farm, was heartbreaking. And of course Patrick was not asked to the reception afterwards, being *persona non grata* as far as the university's reactionary president, Michael Tierney, was concerned: in his view, poetry was all right as long as it was written by distinguished visitors from powerful countries.

When Kavanagh was asked to quit one of the special seats

for the unveiling of the Wolfe Tone statue on the corner of St Stephen's Green opposite the Shelbourne Hotel, because he looked so strange and shabby, his wife Katherine told me that he went home to cry. It was all a mistake, like the failure to invite him to the reception for President John F. Kennedy in the Phoenix Park, but it was the kind of blunder I wanted not to happen again to someone of his calibre. Patrick may now be part of Dublin's cultural tourist industry, with a whimsical statue of him on the Grand Canal and posters bearing his likeness in many of the pubs from which he himself was often barred, but it was painful then to observe his humiliation, despite his weird and wonderful sense of humour, and my impulse was to be as generous to him as I possibly could, without being savaged by his grumpy self. So I do not regret the service to his work that I undertook when I sought to gather his *Collected Poems* from behind the scenes.

COLLECTING KAVANAGH
OR *LATE HARVEST*

At this point I should have another try at telling that story. I
admired Patrick Kavanagh but was wary of him, all the more so
because, coming from an Ulster farming background myself, I
could recognise many of his protective – and destructive –
ploys. When we met alone, things went splendidly, but as soon
as there was an audience, his public personality took over.
Entering John Ryan's Bailey, for example, was like venturing into
the OK Corral. A glance through the swing door would reveal
his massive, dishevelled presence, and I would wait for his salutation. 'Montague, you're a cunt' he would declare with satisfac-
tion. It took me a while to invent the countersign, 'Kavanagh,
you're a hoor.'

If the 'flyting' worked, you were asked to sit down, and
allowed to buy drinks; I was even stood a round several times,
after the calming influence of his marriage. I came in one day
with Terence MacCaughey, then Presbyterian pastor in Trinity
College, who had asked to meet the great man. Patrick savoured
the occasion, warming to an attack, all the sharper because it
involved a fellow Ulsterman. 'Presbyterian – black as the riding
boots of the Earl of Hell!' he announced with relish, and tilted
back. Terence took this in style, and I left them to it. Patrick was,
in his own irreverent way, extremely religious, and was quite
capable of cross-examining Terence on his theological position,
something which he proceeded to do.

But everyone has anecdotes like that about Patrick in the
pub. Maybe I merited a special edge of sharpness as a younger

poet whose name kept cropping up in dispatches. Some of this I understood. He fell into the historical trap which meant that no one of his age and background had more than a glimmer of a chance. Moreover, his achievement was almost all against the grain, a path scythed through the thistles of indifference, the ragwort of a new class of post-revolutionary social climbers. He was also, in a way, a casualty of the Second World War, especially when his publisher, Macmillan, withdrew its support for him. After he moved to Dublin in 1939, there was no way back to the small farm, and no way forward, except for a claustro-phobic office job which, in any case, no one wanted to give him. 'I was a genius, and therefore unemployable,' he would trumpet.

Speaking of office jobs, my easiest time with him was when I lived and worked in the Baggot Street area, a few doors down from where Beatrice and Brendan Behan lived. Patrick and I would cross in Parsons Bookshop, where the ladies reserved him a stool, which he managed to transform into a throne, discoursing with whomever took his fancy, or shambling up to the counter to cash a small cheque or to flirt with the shop girls. Miss O'Flaherty, the owner, was a great support to him. Although a very pious woman, she recognised something almost saintly in Patrick's awkward integrity. She was an intensely dedicated fan, and they were both keen on the horses as well.

There was one splendid afternoon when I slipped out of Bord Fáilte to back a horse called 'Paddy's Point'. I only bet when I am bored, so I was never a true 'affectionado', to use Patrick's phrase. He shuffled into the turf accountants in Haddington Road and was intrigued by my choice. We sat in nearby Mooney's awaiting the result, and when I scored, P.K. was clearly impressed. 'Fancy that now,' he kept repeating. 'A horse with my own name, and Montague wins on it.' Further balls of malt were set up, and we plunged contentedly into a rambling literary discussion, in which it was mutually agreed that, while Goldsmith's *The Deserted Village* had more art than *The Great Hunger*, it had less passion.

When he was at ease like that, the prickliness abated; he could even manage a compliment. When we had met years before, in an earlier incarnation of the Bailey, he was impressed by my dazzling display of foreign tongues. I had asked him out for a meal, and although I was only a gawky young poet, he courteously agreed to come. (I suppose he was famished as well.) When the bill arrived, I asked the French waiter '*si le service est compris?*'

'*Com-pree, com-pree!*' Patrick muttered admiringly. 'Not bad for a Tyrone lad.'

I have tried to remember his occasional kindnesses when dealing myself with the excitable young. Yet I never sought to become part of his circle, except in a tangential way; I was anxious to help, but loath to become a sycophant. In the early 1950s, the *Envoy* days, Patrick was determined to fulfil his public destiny, but the emphasis on his prophetic role made me uneasy. I was well used to country law cases about rights of way and walls and wells – all the usual fuss between neighbours. Had not my Aunt Freda to trek endlessly to Murnaghan's in Omagh over a gate into our mountain pastures, which a neighbour refused to keep closed?

Yet Patrick's outrage at Valentin Iremonger's essay on him in the *Leader*, which led to the infamous libel case, was in excess of the facts. When I read the article aloud, I recognised the voice of the poetry editor of *Envoy*. The details that were provided in the article about everyone's behaviour (including my own) also showed it to be an inside job. 'The three rangy University poets' could only be John Jordan, Anthony Cronin and myself, and 'the redhead' was undoubtedly Clare MacAllister, an ardent, aspiring poet from Grand Rapids, Michigan, who had cascading, auburn hair. So why was Patrick so angry about an article which, though snide in places, was by and large simply literal, a fair enough description of his pub life, and certainly far less critical than his own blasts against his contemporaries?

I would learn later that one should never attempt a libel action unless it is more or less sure to be successful. Since it was clear that Patrick would fail in this crusade, why did he try, especially as everyone knew that the *Leader* had very little money? Either he was spectacularly ill-advised, or else, perhaps unconsciously, he sought a public crucifixion, to expose himself as the outcast artist in a callous society. 'I feel I have the permanent stuff inside me and only need to be stirred,' he once wrote to his brother, but in the absence of any real literary context in which his gift could flourish, he became intent on dramatising himself, to the point where, as Yeats says, a man meets 'the greatest obstacle he can confront without despair'. It was an act of folly akin to Oscar Wilde's libel action, with a brilliant barrister, John A. Costello, future leader of the Irish government, turning the case around against Kavanagh, as Edward Carson had done against Wilde.

It was in the more relaxed atmosphere of the late fifties that we managed to talk more. I was beginning to publish more but didn't dare ask Kavanagh what he thought of it, although when one poem, 'Like Dolmens Round My Childhood', received a small prize, I left a copy of the privately printed edition in Parsons for him. I heard that he had got it, and waited eagerly for the master's comment. Soon afterwards, he halted to speak to me in the street. 'I see you got in the bag apron,' he said gruffly. He went on to speak about authenticity, in the same terms he had used when praising an early essay I had written on William Carleton for *The Bell*, and about how his own mother had worn one of those rough aprons. 'I never managed to get it in meself,' he further offered.

Patrick was intrigued by Thomas Kinsella, whose star was rising rapidly, and was secretly pleased when Tom reviewed *Come*

Dance with Kitty Stobling warmly. 'Do you think he meant it?' he asked me in the pub, scowling over his whiskey. Another time, looking narrowly at Kinsella's bespectacled photograph in the newspaper, after Kinsella had won another prize, Kavanagh growled, 'The eyes. The eyes look inwards,' turning his own great horn-rims towards me. It was a hallucinatory moment, with the thick lenses of both poets seeming to blur before my own eyes.

I am moving back and forward in time because my acquaintance with Kavanagh covered three periods, the *Envoy* days before and up until the law case, the more relaxed period from his convalescence to publication of the *Collected Poems* in 1964, and afterwards, since that volume would be crucial in whatever relationship we finally managed to cobble together between us.

Some years after our occasional leisurely chats in the Baggot Street bars, the phone rang in my exile's hut in Paris. It was my English editor, Timothy O'Keeffe, asking if I would edit Kavanagh's poems for MacGibbon & Kee. Timothy had been present when W. R. Rodgers and I had argued over Kavanagh's merits in the BBC pub, the George. He had carried away the idea – about which, he said, I was very persuasive – of a *Collected*, since most of the poems had been out of print for a long time. The trouble was that Patrick had decided that these earlier poems were dreadful. He was even convinced that his fine, volcanic long poem *The Great Hunger* was tainted by an over-earnest social agenda. As he says in his own short-lived magazine, *Kavanagh's Weekly*, 'Our own misery is never of any importance unless we can take it out and analyse it with detachment.' He had given MacGibbon & Kee a tattered manuscript, but it was only one hundred pages long, and excluded even some of the later work.

I squirmed on the hook, only too aware of the awesome complications that would be involved in such a project. 'What about Anthony Cronin?' I asked, because he had been closer to Patrick than I had ever tried to be, and had done an excellent preface to a selection of Kavanagh's poems for *Nimbus*. I gathered that not only was Cronin far away in Spain, but that he was also out of favour – a name guaranteed to make Kavanagh growl. (Was this a forecast of what was in store for myself?) 'What about John Jordan?' I asked with increasing desperation. Better, but for the fact that, since Jordan was not far away, like Cronin, but a drinking pal of Patrick's in Dublin, Kavanagh was more likely to find out about the project, which might founder as a result. At this point, if I had been concerned merely for myself, I might have given up: Patrick almost invariably forsook those who tried to help him. But Tim argued that my respect for the man's work, without the intensity of a close personal involvement, and the fact that I was a MacGibbon & Kee author, made me the best bet to get the job done, and he knew that he could trust me to be discreet. 'And after all,' he pressed finally, 'this was your idea in the first place!'

There he had me, because O'Keeffe knew my basic concern for the older poet: my desire that he should receive some of the recognition he deserved before it was too late. Kavanagh might scorn the public appeal of a Behan, but I knew that he longed for at least a little of it, especially outside Ireland. Comparing a review I did of *Kitty Stobling* in *Hibernia* with an anonymous encomium in the *Times Literary Supplement*, had he not said 'Yours was the better review, but the other was in a better place'? With grave misgivings, as they say, I consented to help, accepting that my name should be kept out of sight, and even out of print. Martin Green, who would handle the contract, wrote: 'Kavanagh is not the easiest man to deal with on business lines, as you will know, and I think it is fairly important at this stage to keep the selector's name out of sight. . . . I would hasten to add that I don't think he has anything against you, necessarily, but he might against anybody who was in the position with regard to his work that you are in now.'

The only person with whom I discussed my anonymous task was Tom Kinsella, who roundly declared: 'Montague, you're mad! Either get your name openly associated with the edition or don't touch it.' He continued, with prophetic bleakness: 'They don't understand disinterest; they'll attribute the worst possible motives to you.' Alas, he was right, but would Kavanagh's *Collected Poems* have appeared at that time if I had not kept silent? Besides, the work had its own strange rewards for me, like the discovery of two copybooks of verses, some dedicated to a muse called 'Anna Quinn'. I could use only a few of these clumsy yet appealing early poems, or Kavanagh would have been alerted, but they established a frail link between *Ploughman and Other Poems* (1936) and *A Soul for Sale* (1947).

My painter friend Barrie Cooke had unearthed a complete file of the first *Dublin Magazine* and copied out some more early poems from a period when Seamus O'Sullivan, a minor Dublin poet and editor, was one of Kavanagh's few outlets for his work. J. Alan Clodd, a bibliophile and rare-book collector, sent me a typescript of *Ploughman*. Martin Green was supposed to transcribe the Cuala edition of *The Great Hunger* from the copy in the British Museum. However, Martin did not quite understand the importance of restoring the full text from the emasculated version in *A Soul for Sale* (censored, surprisingly, by Kavanagh himself, after the furore over the passages on masturbation in the original edition); as a result, further errors crept in. I would have tackled the transcription myself, but copies of the limited Cuala edition could not, obviously, be found in Paris.

I remember the day I spread the results of my trawls on the floor of our Paris studio. I knew it was incomplete, but time was pressing if we were to do our best by P.K. A chronological edition was out of the question because we did not have the detailed information required to establish each poem's provenance, or the time to amass such information. Even to arrange the work by volumes was difficult, because of the erratic nature of his career: there was only one commercial publication, *Come Dance with Kitty Stobling*, during fifteen years of work. With some reluctance, I tried to arrange the later poems in a pattern corresponding to what I understood of Kavanagh's progress since *A Soul for Sale*: from satire to confession, and finally acceptance. (Only one reviewer, Douglas Hyde's erudite and courteous nephew Douglas Sealy, understood the pattern I was trying to discern. He analyses this in, once again, the *Dublin Magazine*, though under a later editorship.) I thought of adding Kavanagh's splendid essay 'From Monaghan to the Grand Canal' as a Preface, but Patrick himself came up with a few sharp words for the occasion.

And occasion it was – the kind of party that Patrick must have dreamed of, with Black Velvet (a luscious but potent mix of champagne and stout) flowing in the Guinness mansion in Mayfair. I had met one of my favourite English poets, William Empson, in Hampstead that morning, and asked him to come along; he and Kavanagh got on famously, after Patrick's informal salutation, 'How ya, Bill', as if he had always known him.

It was on that night I became aware of how much his future wife, Katherine, loved Kavanagh. After the party (which ended abruptly when two poets began to demonstrate rugby passes with bottles of champagne), we tumbled into a local Henekeys pub, a ragged army. When the publican tried to upbraid Kavanagh for his bedraggled appearance, Katherine came to his rescue, putting the publican firmly in his place. Later, while a tired but pleased Patrick was drooping at the bus stop, she looked protectively towards his shabby bulk. 'There goes all of God I shall know in this life,' she said to me with grave tenderness.

The rest we know: the featured review by A. Alvarez in the

Observer, and general acclaim in places like the *Spectator* (by a for-giving Frank O'Connor), the *New Statesman* and the *New York Times*. With three years left to live, Kavanagh saw most of his work coming back into print: my backstage effort had worked. I would like to think that all this eased things a little for him. The young adored him: he was the kingpin of new literary magazines like James Liddy's *Arena* and Brian Lynch's *The Holy Door* – 'King of the Kids', as Brendan Behan amusedly described him. And Kavanagh himself must have been pleased, since he had declared, in vatic mode: 'Not to be exciting to the young is death!'

(It is wrong, by the way, to presume that Behan did not admire Kavanagh as a writer; for him, only Máirtín Ó Cadháin and Flann O'Brien were on the same level as Kavanagh, and he would have been glad to have settled their differences if Patrick had been willing to do so. Having acted as an intermediary, pass-ing notes between the two supposed antagonists as if we were all furtive schoolboys, I can testify that Brendan was prepared to make it up, and to help Kavanagh financially or otherwise if he could. Although Brendan had probably helped to produce a damning piece of evidence during the libel action – a copy of *Tarry Flynn* inscribed to 'My friend, Brendan' – it was because Kavanagh had betrayed him in public, declaring, from the dock, that they had never been friends.)

With all his talk of courtesy, Patrick could be unforgiving, even vicious, about fellow (usually Irish) writers. When I came into McDaids one day, Patrick looked up from the racing page and asked in his brusque fashion, 'Any news? What's stirring?'

I obliged him by saying, 'Frank O'Connor is very ill. He's just had a heart attack.'

'Good news! Good news!' enthused Patrick.

I was shocked, and told him so. He took my rebuke serious-ly, agreeing that it was not a nice attitude, but that I was too young to understand why one would relish banishing people to hell, as Dante had done. It was on this occasion that he explained to me that only the English poet George Barker understood obscenity as deeply as himself. I had a glimpse of the loneliness, frustration and rage through which Kavanagh had often had to plough.

His abrasive humour often had an element of the philosophical. On another occasion, I came into McDaids with the veteran American writer Nelson Algren to find Patrick at the bar, engaged in matters of high finance with the legendary barman, Paddy O'Brien, who looked after all the literary hard cases with considerable aplomb. (According to Paddy, 'If this lot would give up the drink, they'd have the beatings of the world in writing.' But then he would have been out of a job!) Patrick was signing a cheque, but very slowly, because he was writing his name in Irish, a language he usually disdained. 'This way, it'll take longer to clear,' he explained. 'As you will doubtless learn, Montague, life is a matter of lodging and checking.'

I tried to translate this aphorism into Americanese for Algren, who had never heard of Kavanagh, just as Kavanagh had never heard of him. Nelson was disposed to be friendly, however, and he tried to find common ground in a neutral topic. Like everyone else at the time, he had been reading a long article in *Life* magazine about the declining population of Ireland in the 1950s due to late marriages. It was a polemical piece by Seán O'Faolain, whom I knew Patrick had grown to dislike, roughly for the same reason that he disliked O'Connor: for what he considered a falsification of Irish life by writers who were no longer in touch with it. But Patrick chose to take a more general view of the situation, perhaps scenting some sport – or possibly a snort of whiskey in the offing.

'And what do you think, Mr Kavanagh, of this idea that the Irish are vanishing?' asked Algren politely.

Patrick's eyes glinted behind the thick horn-rims. 'Too good to be true,' he delivered, tilting backwards and forwards on his phantom rocking chair, and laughing. 'Too good to be true.' And off he went into further bursts of laughter.

Algren took the cue, and drinks were set up. As he negotiated at the bar, Kavanagh leaned across to me and murmured conspiratorially, 'I know he's a writer. But what does he write about? Tell me quick before he comes back.'

I gave a swift, potted version of Algren's career, the stumble-bums and prostitutes of old-style Chicago and New Orleans, as depicted in *Never Come Morning*, *The Neon Wilderness*, *A Walk on the Wild Side* and, of course, *The Man with the Golden Arm*. Expressionless, with folded arms, Kavanagh absorbed my dispatch. 'But does he have the readies?' he whispered urgently.

'A bit more than us,' I answered, as Nelson returned with two glasses of whiskey, for himself and Patrick, and a Guinness for me. They moved around each other gingerly, like boxers from different countries, feeling out each other's style. Patrick was in a good mood, even more so by the time he got on to the second whiskey, and soon they fell on a topic common to them both: horse racing, betting, bookies and their touts. Algren was intrigued by the term 'turf accountant', which Patrick said should equally apply to most Irish writing. He tried to explain that O'Faolain was too polite to fathom the street life of modern Dublin; then a thought seemed to strike him. 'Montague tells me you write well about whores. I know they have them in Chicago and the Wild West, but d'you know that we have them here, too?' Patrick tilted his head discreetly towards the counter. 'See that woman up there, alone at the bar? She's on the game. I'm sure she'd be glad to meet an American writer like yourself.'

She was a fairly well-dressed, middle-aged woman, with one of the demure hairstyles of that period, short and blonde. I had seen her in the bar a few times before; she was friendly with one of the painters who frequented McDaids. All in all, she looked like a pleasant, middle-class Dublin lady on her office break. So imagine how startled she looked as Algren surged up behind her, tapped her on the shoulder, and made his outrageous proposition. Kavanagh and I could see her face as she ran through the gamut of emotions, from puzzlement, to incredulity, to anger, as an oblivious Algren reached into his pocketbook to show her some greenbacks. Then she spied Patrick over his shoulder, heaving with wheezy laughter, and began to laugh herself.

I don't think Algren quite got the joke, but he and Kavanagh continued to talk comfortably, and in his travel book *Who Lost An American?* Algren records his admiration for Kavanagh in glowing terms (even if some of them had been lifted from a review in the *TLS*, not a magazine one would expect a tough Chicagoan to read). He does not mention the incident with the lady in McDaids, however.

*

As well as helping with the *Collected Poems*, I played a minor part in the production of Patrick's Claddagh record *Almost Everything*, in my weighty capacity as (honorary) speech director and founding member of that august firm. Although this was our first speech record, I kept out of sight, for by now I was also out of favour – if I ever had been in. Whether Kavanagh had got wind of my part in the *Collected Poems* I do not know, but clearly he had decided that I was up to no good. Wherever he turned, he seemed to find me: first at MacGibbon & Kee and now at Claddagh, preparing a sleeve note for *Almost Everything*, albeit prudently signed only with my initials.

Worst of all, my short-story collection *Death of a Chieftain* appeared a few months after his *Collected*, and got warm reviews – extracts from which were quoted in MacGibbon & Kee's publicity brochures. Warm, that is, except for one, a swingeing tirade by Patrick in *Hibernia*, which was more a bull charge than a review. I briefly replied, which I probably should not have done; worse, several people came sharply to my defence. Frustrated by what seemed to be another example of rank Irish ingratitude, I began to understand what he meant about himself and Frank O'Connor: the air between us had grown too thick with static for any communication.

If this wasn't enough to get his hackles up, I wrote a deliberately provocative summary of recent Irish verse for an American magazine, in which I praised Patrick's 'honesty of vision' as liberating. However, I went on to declare that 'It has liberated us into ignorance: he has literally nothing to say.' This was meant to define the way he had freed us from the Celtic Twilight, but he interpreted it as simple malice, not an attempt to get at the truth. I did not mean 'iggerance' in the Ballyrush Bottom or Garvaghey Gougers' club football sense. I meant it in the sense of not knowing: not knowing how to husband his energy, not knowing friend from foe, not knowing where to turn in literature or life to renew his resources, in the void of post-Emergency Dublin. One of his very last poems contains that blend of splendour and bleakness which was exactly what my essay was driving at:

> What am I to do
> With the void growing more awful every hour?
> I lacked a classical discipline. I grew
> Uncultivated and now the soil turns sour . . .

Patrick never seemed to realise, however, that very few of his generation of poets, anywhere, had it easy. Louis MacNeice, his younger contemporary, died before him, a release preferable to the nursery reversion of Kavanagh's idol, W. H. Auden. John Hewitt and Austin Clarke were virtually unknown outside Ireland, and Padraic Fallon had yet to publish a book.

Even more savage was the plight of the Americans, whom Kavanagh scorned in toto, without trying to understand their efforts. Theodore Roethke had passed through Dublin in the early sixties, with a sheaf of marvellous nature poems, the nucleus of *The Far Field*, as wild and lovely a book as Patrick's own *Kitty Stobling*. Roethke had fame and love at last, but he was shattered with drink, and haunted by death, which came to him in 1963, so that *The Far Field* was published posthumously. A few years later, John Berryman arrived in Dublin to finish his *Dream Songs*. He was eager to meet Kavanagh, but it could not be arranged, although, through Katherine, I got our grumpy bard to attend the farewell reading that I had organised for Berryman. Patrick flounced out early, on what seemed to me a pretext (a glancing mention of Liam Miller by Berryman); he apologised afterwards – a rare occurrence for him. I gather that the two men did finally meet, in the Royal Albert Hall. Berryman was an even greater master of the sonnet sequence as a means of spiritual exploration: they should have had much to roar about before they went down.

Largely through the good offices of Katherine, as on the Berryman occasion, we managed a corrida-like exchange, as described earlier. But Kavanagh never understood that his suffering and isolation were part of the exhausted post-war, post-Modernist atmosphere in which poets sang and died like flies, with only the wily, like the English poet George Barker, or the scholarly, like the American Stanley Kunitz, escaping. Kavanagh was nearly alone in his extreme poverty, however; there, again, his reappearance in print helped. Public engagements followed, at last, like the Albert Hall Poetry International, where he found himself among his (also dying) peers: Berryman, Pablo Neruda and Giuseppe Ungaretti. And then there was the Arts Council Award: the British Arts Council, alas – but that would have pleased him, with his illusion that London was a centre of literary integrity. Ironically, the Irish Arts Council passed over his *Collected Poems* for the Denis Devlin Award, giving it instead to a very slim volume by Kinsella, *Wormwood*. I found this decision shockingly insensitive: half a dozen polished poems by a young and successful poet, as opposed to the life's work of a great but still very poor man. But Paddy's comment on the matter showed an increasing composure with regard to his younger contemporaries. I did not bring it up when we met in the Bailey, but after a while he lifted his gaze from the sports pages: 'Did you see that Kinsella won the Davis Cup?' Like the bag apron, you could take it both ways. I prefer to regard it as a victory: regal indifference had won the day.

It was astonishing to me, as a Northerner, how my contemporaries at University College Dublin seemed already aware of the positions they might occupy in their fairly new State. Quite a few of their parents were civil war veterans who had pursued careers in law or economics, since they had been eager to mould their own social structures and draft their own laws after centuries of English rule. Their sons and daughters, my fellow students, were choosing the same areas of study, but for a different reason. It was as if they instinctively understood that in this new, flourishing Catholic republic, certain powerful positions would automatically materialise for them.

My Uncle Tom had kept a tiny faded photograph of a man he said was the first attorney general of the Irish Free State, and several of those who would become his successors were scattered among my fellow students at university, like the hapless P. J. Connelly. Future judges and government ministers were preening themselves around me, using the Law Society and the famous Literary and Historical Society as training grounds for their youthful eloquence.

Although UCD was mainly a Fine Gael university, there was a group of young Fianna Fáil bloods centred on the Commerce Society, including the stubby figure of Charles Haughey and the eternally affable Brian Lenihan. But they were marginal figures to me, obsessed as I was with my artistic quest, which involved me with the odd men out, the bohemians like Anthony Cronin and Pearse Hutchinson. They were already rebelling against this embryonic society of power and privilege, which they, unlike myself, had seen develop – a well-fed phoenix soaring slowly from the ashes of insurrection and civil war. I admired their defiant spirit, but how could I protest against a society I did not understand? My own father and uncles, who should have been part of it, had taken flight as far as England, America and even Australia, such was the effect of Partition on Catholic men of the North.

So instead of prospering in the new State for which they had fought, they scattered, and I was left with absence and incomprehension as my patrimony, in a North where Catholics felt betrayed and abandoned by Partition, and for whom Dublin was, in more ways than one, another country. In the pre-Treaty North, my maternal uncles had both been in the original IRA, and afterwards in the Irish army – which they later left in disgust, feeling that they were being conscripted to exact revenge in Southern civil conflicts about which they knew nothing. Not only did they find themselves fighting to defend Partition, a concept they loathed; they were also being recruited to execute those who opposed it, men from the South whom they did not know personally but whom they would have regarded as comrades. So, despite my patriotic antecedents, it was not easy for me to step into the post-Treaty society in which I found myself.

I really met Charles Haughey for the first time at a select dinner in an opulent private house. The cast of characters included a surprising number of those we would now call 'movers and shakers'. Our best-known architect, Michael Scott, was there, along with his pal Father Donal O'Sullivan, SJ, director of the Arts Council. (Father O'Sullivan was acting like a Trojan horse in that sedate institution, smuggling a great deal of modern, often abstract, art into the Irish consciousness, and also onto the walls of the Arts Council's offices on Merrion Square.) Also present was C. S. (Todd) Andrews, who had moved from his position as commissar of Bord na Móna, the Irish Turf Board (as in fuel, not horse racing), to CIÉ, which was responsible for the Irish public-transport system. Although I was acquainted with a number of these guests, it was Madeleine whom they really knew, and they liked her for her vivacity and intelligence, as well as the fact that she was an exotic Parisienne.

Haughey had the place of honour, as Minister of Finance, and the table was laden with the fine wines of which he professed to be a connoisseur. After a few glasses had slid silkily down our throats, Haughey turned the searchlight of his attention towards me. He clearly had not the faintest notion as to why I was there, and could barely even place me. He had, however, registered that I had a Northern accent, and Madeleine a charming French one.

The general conversation had begun in the usual way of genteel Dublin dinner parties, with a discussion of recent plays at the Abbey and Gate Theatres. Michael Scott contributed a particular analysis of acoustics, since, in an earlier incarnation, he had been a minor Abbey actor, under the predatory name of 'Wolfe'. The plays of Alderman McCann, the father of the actor Donal, had been having some success at the Abbey, which was still exiled to its temporary billet in the Queen's while the new theatre was being built. At one point, Mrs Haughey piped up plaintively: 'I don't see why there's all this fuss about O'Casey. I think John McCann's plays are much better. At least I enjoy them more than O'Casey's gloomy stories about those slums.'

Todd Andrews laughed. 'I take your point, Mrs Haughey. I'm from nearly the same neighbourhood myself.'

Encouraged, she asked: 'And wasn't O'Casey a Protestant? How would he know about those people?'

Todd laughed again. 'Indeed! Who ever heard of a poor Protestant?'

Minister Haughey had been surveying the table through hooded eyes. 'Never mind her,' he said brusquely, with a dismissive wave in his wife's direction. 'She knows nothing about art.'

Embarrassed, we moved away from theatre to discuss the early days of the State's economic growth, through companies like Todd's Bord na Móna, as well as the electrification scheme on the Shannon, and later on the Erne at Ballyshannon. Todd told many amusing anecdotes as to how the German and Russian technicians always gave, and expected, presents – a practice to which the idealistic young Irish former gunmen were completely unaccustomed. These zealous republicans might have learnt to kill, but they recoiled like virgins from the sight of a brown envelope, which they spurned with lofty harshness – until they realised that their scorn was interfering with business.

Madeleine chimed in, explaining how her tough-minded younger brother, Philippe, had said that there was no government official in France you could not influence by placing a discreet envelope on his desk. If he slid it open and seemed pleased with the contents, absorbing it into his files, your plea would eventually be heard. If it stayed on the desk, you were lost, and must know to whisk it away. This practice prevailed even in banks, Madeleine assured us.

'You're a bright one,' said Haughey admiringly. 'You seem to know how the world works. People like Todd here thought that truth lay in the barrel of a gun. That's necessary sometimes, but there are other ways of persuasion.' Then a thought seemed to strike him, and he turned to me, lofting a full glass. 'I can hear that you're from the North. But from which side of what we have to call "the border"?'

I gazed at him across the table – those shrewd, narrowed eyes; that blunt face, like a hammer-headed shark. He was intimidating all right, but everyone present had been assembled to please him, because of some necessary deal: I think it was the rebuilding of the Abbey Theatre, which was probably exceeding its budget. And of course the grant for the Arts Council depended on the Minister for Finance. So although I was beginning to find Haughey truculent and abrasive, and had been shocked by his show of disdain for his wife, I felt that I should not upset the apple cart, especially since Madeleine, who had also registered his sullenness, was teasing him gently.

So I gave him a quick summary of my family background, stressing the various individuals' involvement in the national struggle, but not their disillusionment after Partition. My Uncle Frank, a medical student, was supposed to have been in the same regiment as Kevin Barry, and according to my mother was one of Michael Collins' men, and had been at the Russell Hotel on that first Bloody Sunday morning. I could see no connection, however, between these stories of military prowess and the plump, flannel-sheathed, tennis-playing doctor who visited us on summer holidays accompanied by Stan, his equally stylish English pal.

Frank had a prospering practice in Chester, though I never visited him there, and was too young to get to know him well before he died in the England he had fought against. When I was at Yale, however, I did visit my Uncle Tom Carney, now a superintendent of the Interborough Rapid Transit, or subway. In his flat New York accent, he told me how he had been a sharpshooter for the Irish army – which I could well believe, because he had struck the targets at the funfair in Bundoran with such precision and regularity that the exasperated proprietor had finally asked him not to come any more. His favourite story was how, when anti-Treaty forces were besieging Dundalk, he had been deputed to kill Frank Aiken, but had just missed him. I told Aiken this story years afterwards, and he was deeply amused. 'So that was your uncle. I remember I moved at the last second, and the bullet burned along the side of my head.'

I told Haughey that my mother's family, the Carneys, had inherited a souvenir book from the internment camp at Ballykinlar in County Down. Uncle Frank had been there, along with Haughey's father-in-law, Seán Lemass, a future Taoiseach –

like Haughey himself. My Uncle Frank did not take to the Dubliner Lemass, however, because – ironically, considering his name – he did not attend Mass, something which was shocking to a patriotic Ulster Catholic for whom religion and national identity had become nearly the same thing. (But not surprising to me, considering that the IRA had been excommunicated en bloc.) Yet Lemass seemed always to know that he would overcome. Among the coy and pious sentiments inscribed in the souvenir book (similar to those in the little albums from my Armagh school years), one verse stood out: that of Seán F. Lemass. Unlike the others, there were no references to the Sacred Heart, the Blessed Virgin, or Holy Ireland, just a confident declaration: 'I'd like to bet/ I'll come home yet/ With a brass band/ Playing before.'

Yet despite such occasional droll anecdotes, it seemed to me a sad story that I was telling, even though I tried to sweeten it with descriptions of rural Tyrone, and the strangeness of backwaters like Fintona. But only one thing seemed to interest Haughey.

'Tell me,' he said, those heavy hooded eyes appraising me again, 'how does a boyo from the Clogher valley manage to get his hands on a bird from Paris?'

There was a collective intake of breath, yet no one said a word: no one but Madeleine, that is. With her customary broad grin, she replied: 'Because he's good-looking. Besides, he's bright, and writes pretty well.'

'Oh, so he's a writer,' said Haughey slowly, undeflected. 'I know lots of writers. There's always one or two of them waiting outside the door, hoping to have a word with me.'

Keeping my cool with an effort, I widened my eyes in a pretence of curiosity, and asked: 'Really? What are the names of these writers?'

As I expected, he produced the names of only a few journalists: decent folk whose commentaries I followed, but none of whom had ever written a book. 'I think you are confusing journalists with what we call creative writers,' I responded patiently. 'You know what I mean, or at least you should. People like Patrick Kavanagh: you must have followed his unfortunate court case. And then there's Austin Clarke, who is as poor as a church mouse. In fact, why is there not a Civil List for people like that, the way there is in England? They're too poor to even exile themselves! But you must know all this.'

Haughey fell silent, brooding. The dinner party seemed to have collapsed, poisoned by these unexpectedly rough exchanges. The irrepressible Michael Scott managed to shift the conversation to the subject of wines, and soon he and Haughey were debating the better years of claret. It was clear that they were not burgundy men, as they extolled, with an almost salacious relish, the 'full body' and 'rounded texture' of a certain Bordeaux. Michael was a past master at pleasing, at drawing the best out of, people, with his small glittering eyes and wide smile, but even he must have felt that the evening had failed, or at least had taken a wrong turn somewhere.

Before Haughey left, I found myself briefly alone with him, in a room with fine paintings by Irish artists. 'I can understand that stuff,' he said gruffly, 'but I'm not sure what you're going on about. I know your uncles weren't very bright, if they didn't stay to reap the benefit of the new State. Ideals are grand, but they can be too costly. My father was from Swatragh, in Derry, and that's only a step above Fintona. We need people from the North down here; the problem's still not solved, and it's bound to come up again. And this Dublin lot don't know or care enough – it all seems far away to them. And that Cork lot know nothing except themselves.'

*

100

A week later, when I was in my favourite Dublin bookshop, Hodges Figgis on Dawson Street, the manager came hurrying over to me. 'You'll be glad to know you have a new reader. There was somebody in from Minister Haughey's office, to buy all your books: I didn't know your man was an admirer of poetry.'

Whether he read them or not, whenever I met Mr Haughey again, in or out of office, he always offered me a drink, or slid one along the bar, with the same sly query: 'How's the poetry going?' I met him once after he'd lost an election, and I asked: 'What will you do now?'

'Enjoy myself,' he smiled, clasping the hand of the tall lady painter beside him.

During the late 1960s, Haughey became friendly with the idealistically patriotic Seán Ó Riada, composer of 'Mise Éire'. I took no part in their conspiratorial exchanges, but Haughey cleared a space for me beside him at Seán's funeral. Much later, he consulted me about a poem or blessing for the opening of Knock Airport, an Irish version of Lourdes. I was glad to pass this task on to Paul Durcan, who was from those parts. Durcan's poem for the occasion turned out to be a sonorous litany of place names, but that is another story.

Trying to fathom the complex character of Charles Haughey, who was so extraordinarily capable but also so coarse, like the cliché of the rough-spoken, cigar-chomping Boss Tweed of New York's Tammany Hall, I was helped by a meeting with one of the most distinguished older Irishmen, called, indeed, John de Courcy Ireland. John had tackled Haughey head-on about the mishandling of and ignorance about maritime matters in Ireland, but Haughey had, in effect, told this courteous, elderly gentleman to 'Fuck off'. Haughey later summoned him to his office for a detailed conference on the issues raised and, said John, was the first politician really to try to tackle the problem. We agreed to recognise that Haughey belonged to a particular breed of Irishman, an irrepressible 'slagger' – one who needs to excoriate you before he can befriend you, and then settle down to business.

During my mid-sixties campaign in Dublin, Madeleine came over, of course, to stay in Anglesea Street, or I would fly back to Paris. We sometimes had wonderful long weekends above Rathfarnham, at Woodtown Manor, which had been the home of the painter Morris Graves and now belonged to our friend Garech Browne, the founder of Claddagh Records. Yet wild parties and music in the Dublin hills could not obscure the fact that the city was changing; when I looked through my high, sooty Anglesea Street windows over central Dublin, I could see cranes everywhere, razing venerable Georgian houses and throwing up sub-Bauhaus blocks in their place.

Another change was that my own creative generation was dispersing, even enduring its first untimely death. Brendan Behan had died during my second teaching year in Berkeley: he had drunk himself underground. I missed his almost Wildean wit and unpredictable behaviour as I moved through our altered city. Anthony Cronin had left with his family for Spain, where he could live more cheaply. Even Tom Kinsella, my favourite poetic sparring partner, was preparing to leave the Department of Finance, and teach in some distant American university: who had ever heard of Carbondale? And, in a dramatic gesture, my doppelgänger, John Jordan, editor of *Poetry Ireland*, had determined to exile himself all the way to Newfoundland: who had ever heard of St John's? Richard Murphy was building his rose-red villa in the West, while John MacGahern's life was changing through his collision with the Censorship Board and the loss of his teaching job. So it seemed that I was coming back to a city that my contemporaries were intent on leaving, voyaging into various forms of exile, to echo a title of my own.

Despite this exodus, however, a new, younger group had emerged, more loosely connected to UCD. A fairly bohemian lot, some would be nourished by the later Kavanagh: like the rebelly Paul Durcan; the darkly handsome Macdara Woods; and the slight, impish Michael Hartnett with his shining brown eyes beneath luxuriant brows, and his intense lyric gift. This younger poetic scene was sustained by broadsheets, usually launched with readings attended by relatives, and girlfriends and boyfriends. The amiable Hayden Murphy hawked his broadsheets around the pubs, and the then leading student poet at UCD, Richard Ryan, did the same. Skinny, with his leather bomber jacket and motorcycle, Richard looked more like James Dean than the distinguished diplomat he would become, in our embassy in London, as well as points east and west – Korea, Japan and New York. He had a taut, nervous talent, but had he the staying power to ripen into a real poet? I suppose that now we may never know, since the disciplines of the diplomatic service draw on the same psychic energies one might otherwise husband for the jealous muse. Still, *Ledges* and *Ravenswood* were a promising start, and he shared a Faber Introduction with a precociously talented young poet from the North, Paul Muldoon.

To enliven matters, I began a poetry-reading series in the little Lantern Theatre, almost below the British Embassy on Merrion Square, with the help, again, of Liam Miller. Retrospectively, I think we achieved a lot, including Seamus Heaney's Dublin debut, and bringing over some of my poetic pals from Paris like Michel Deguy and Serge Fauchereau, to suggest a different and more exacting aesthetic. (I played some of the harsher music of Boulez during the intervals, to the surprise of the Dublin audience.) The Lantern Theatre was a wonderful little space, often with a very distinguished though small audience, assembled by Liam Miller himself, who, with his dark beard and sloe eyes, was a perfect Hiberno-Hebraic type, like the poet Kinsella, who had described himself wittily once as 'ancient, Jew-face law'. Sometimes, seeing them together, I recalled with amusement the old canard about Israel being one of the lost tribes of Ireland. The climax of the season, in more ways than one, was the farewell reading of John Berryman, on the completion of the *Dream Songs*, his immense sonnet sequence – longer, indeed, than those of any of the Elizabethans he loved to invoke.

Liam Miller's enthusiasm about the Berryman reading, as well as all the other Lantern performances, was a heartening thing. He was a genius in his own way, a provincial dynamo or Dublin Diaghilev, pullulating with plans for poetry and publication. And of course those beautifully produced books, some of which would be launched at the Lantern, were tumbling from his press. He had me phoning the Russian embassy in London in order to have a Russian delegation for a great extravaganza of poetry, which we agreed to call 'Fleadh na bFilí', which means 'Festival of the Poets' in Irish but sounds like 'Feast of the Billy Goats'. It was meant to be a bardic festival to match the music festivals that had begun to bring rural Ireland to life. My old boss, Tim O'Driscoll, director general of Bord Fáilte, underwrote the series, with his typical enterprising spirit (which I had already celebrated in my short story 'A Change of Management').

Like myself, Liam saw bohemia as an alternative family, and when his wife was away, nothing would do him but that we should descend into Dublin's literary underworld. One evening stands out in my mind. It was Saturday night, and the air in the pub was thick with smoke, the smell of porter, and what the Scots call 'flytings' – ritual exchanges of insults among equals. Kavanagh was holding court in a corner (although his head was beginning to droop a little), admirers crowded around a slender

Egyptian girl everyone called Cleopatra, and the sculptor Frank Morris was revving up to one of his revelations. Accompanying him was the gifted artist Camille Souter, with her rakish beret and generous smile.

I enjoyed these forays into 'night town', since I had no family home in Dublin to harbour me after my day's labours, teaching and writing, no kindly aunt or cousin to allay the loneliness. The Dublin publican's appeal at closing time was not the sedate 'Drink up, gentlemen; it's time' of T. S. Eliot's London, but 'Ah, come on, lads, have yiz no homes to go to?' – a challenge which I found plaintive, having indeed no home to go to. And I imagine that Patrick Kavanagh, during the lean years before his marriage, must have felt the same.

Yet despite the allure of pub as womb, masculine drinking expeditions were neither wise, practical nor possible except now and again, so that, to my dismay, the pattern of dalliance that I had left Berkeley to break was reasserting itself, as an alternative to the bottle. I might have come back to Europe, where I was closer to Madeleine and Paris, but I was still mainly leading a bachelor's life in a bachelor flat, cooking up forlorn meals of bacon and eggs while I listened to the radio, or prepared the next day's lecture. One Sunday night, sleepless, I finally clambered out of bed at four in the morning and wrote to Madeleine. 'I don't seem to be able to sleep, or rather the night seems to be bringing me more truth than I can bear, so I get up to write to you. That is the real root of loneliness, not to have the one person to whom one seems to be able to explain most things . . . physically present. To speak on the phone is not enough.' Sometimes, when the loneliness pressed too heavily, I would venture into the Trocadero restaurant, a Dublin version of New York's Sardi's, with its masculine décor and photographs of actors, some of whom would saunter in at a late hour.

When I needed feminine company, I took Nuala O'Faolain to see boxing matches – almost my favourite sport – at the

106

National Stadium. I admired her lecturing skills, which made her nearly the most popular member of staff in the English Department at UCD; she would control the boys in the back of the hall by shifting a saucy skirt to catch their attention.

And then, reluctantly and ruefully, I began a light liasion with a sweet, shy young Dublin woman. I enjoyed her gentleness and relative innocence, but I had to tread carefully, for although she loved the company of writers, she tended to idealise them, knowing little about either them or their sometimes harsh bohemian world. For example, I was loath to expose her to the hurly-burly of McDaids, where her romantic image of writers would surely be tarnished. I was disappointed but almost relieved when she sought a job outside Ireland, which would mean that she would be absent when I next returned to Dublin. After abandoning Berkeley to revive my marriage, I certainly did not want to get in too deep, or to cause harm. Nevertheless, I began a poem as a tentative homage to the sweetness of our encounters, in which I also tried to convey some of the wistfulness inherent in a relationship that is, by its nature, evanescent. Though explicit, it is meant to be a tender poem, which explores the contrast between an experience of intimacy and the neutral territory in which it might, incongruously, take place:

> I shall miss you
> creaks the mirror
> into which the scene
> will shortly disappear:
> the vast bedroom
> a hall of air, the
> tracks of our bodies
> fading there, while
> giggling maids push
> a trolley of fresh
> linen down the corridor.

> I have moved to Dublin to have it out with you,
> majestic Shade . . .

Few people realise that John Berryman's *Dream Songs* were completed in Ireland, but since I was in attendance as occasional midwife, a few notes on that difficult delivery may be in order, especially since I already knew Berryman, from a previous existence.

The first background against which I saw John was the State University of Iowa. 'Detestable state,' he growls in 'Dream Song 290', composed as 'the great boat moves on' towards Ireland, which is, by contrast, an

> Adorable country, in its countryside
> & persons, & its habits, & its past,
> martyrs & heroes,
> its noble monks, its wild men of high pride
> & poets long ago, Synge, Joyce & Yeats,
> and the ranks from which they rose.

In Iowa I was, of course, hoping to study with Berryman, but he seemed to be ostentatiously spurning poetry, teaching an academic course on the short story and sharing the Fiction Workshop. Puzzled, I decided that he was probably determined to bring the talent flickering in his short story 'The Imaginary Jew' to fulfilment, whereas what had really happened was that Paul Engle was hugging the Poetry Workshop to himself. (Engle was Iowa's unofficial laureate, and founding father of the famous Writing Programme. But he was a tense and bitter man, whose appalling and unfortunately titled *Corn* had got the Pulitzer prize just as such mawkish down-home sentiment was going out of fashion.)

It was very noticeable that Berryman was always alone: one saw him eating alone at the Jefferson Hotel, or stalking alone into the cinema. And in the evenings he was invariably in a bar near the university – the famous Kenney's, where all the sensitive plants went to be watered. He would hunch up on a stool, book open before him on the counter, his rebarbative shoulders forbidding conversation. And it was there that some kind of confrontation took place. Apparently some student had addressed him in too familiar a fashion, breezily calling, 'Hiya, John! How ya doin'?' with a clap on the back, which was brusquely thrown off. 'Professor Berryman to you, sir,' was the frosty reply, leading to a flurry of ineffectual blows, after which a further scuffle took place between a distraught Berryman and his landlord. John landed in the town jail.

Being thrown in the slammer is not unusual among writers, but they are not usually attached to universities, and do not generally find themselves exposed in the morning newspaper. Still, I was surprised when Berryman did not show up for class: my youthful hero-worship did not make allowance for how a university administration might regard such wayward behaviour. Unbeknownst to us, Paul Engle had called Berryman to inform him that the Dean and Provost had summoned him. Whether Berryman was sacked, or resigned, the result was the same: he left Iowa for Minnesota, where his friend Allen Tate would 'welcome me properly', John said.

All this would have little relevance if the incident had not helped to provoke some kind of change in Berryman; or so it seemed to me. The man I met in Iowa was taut, arrogant, as nervous as a star pitcher: very nearly a caricature of the fiercely defensive intellectual of the fifties. Hair-triggered for insult, a poet determined to outdo the scholars, he was, at that time, capable of coming to blows with a mere student. Whereas the man I re-met in Dublin was very nearly the reverse – enthusiastic, hilarious, as splendid and generous a figure as one might meet, fitting into the roar of Dublin pub life with ease. Or rather for whom the city's pub life was a natural backdrop, not for reading but for writing; the move from the literary salon meant that many public houses had grown accustomed to writers as ordinary working people, spreading their papers like any student or intellectual in a bustling Paris café. Except that the pub was more dangerous, since, instead of a thimble of coffee or a modest glass of wine, one took whiskey or Guinness. Brian O'Nolan, alias Myles na gCopaleen, alias Flann O'Brien, often composed his *Irish Times* column in that atmosphere of intense privacy which can sometimes be achieved in a very public place, and of course Kavanagh and Behan were often to be seen in the hostelries.

What I mainly want to convey is my delight in the man who now glowed with a kind of wild, bearded benignity. He had written from Minnesota asking if I could find him a house in Dublin, but since I had returned to Paris for the mid-term break, I suggested that he stay at the Majestic Hotel in Upper Fitzwilliam Street until Liam Miller and I could help him find a place. So for a short time he and his family stayed in that rather dingy hotel in the centre of Dublin, just across the road from the raffish Arts Club, with its eternally open bar – to which we took care not to introduce him, lest he get lost forever. Anyway, the large lounge of the Majestic was womb enough from home, the scene of many memorable conversations well fuelled by a variety of drinks, although Berryman stuck to his American guns, eschewing everything but spirits.

> Henry is feeling better,
> owing to three gin-&-vermouths.
> He is seeking where to live and pursue his work.

Yet soon enough we did indeed help him find a house of his own, a bleak semi-detached in Ballsbridge, but with an excellent old-fashioned pub nearby, Jack Ryan's of Beggar's Bush, into which he could slip to work. And further along there was Slattery's, another splendid establishment, in case he felt lonely: 'the Irish sun comes back & forth, and I/ in my Irish pub/ past puberty and into pub-erty . . . '.

The locals enjoyed him, and encouraged his exuberant scribbles, with shouts of 'Give us another blast of a ballad, John!' Berryman was the only writer I have ever seen for whom drink seemed a positive stimulus. He drank enormously and smoked heavily, but it seemed apart of a pattern of work, a crashing through the barriers as he raced towards the completion of the *Dream Songs*, sometimes three or four a day. He seemed positively happy, a man engaged in completing his masterwork, with a wife and child he adored. He had come into his own, and radiated the psychic electricity of genius; that some of the newer *Songs* seemed to be rubbish meant merely that they were part of this volcanic overflow. He delighted in talking about literature, which he clearly loved with an all-absorbing passion. He would cry while reciting the Paolo and Francesca episode from *The Inferno*, or suddenly leap up to shake the hand of Denis Donoghue, because they agreed about the merits of a particular Henry James story. He was no longer concerned with appearances, as his long, hacking coughs halted his conversation, or his increasingly wild gestures sent a glass flying:

> Hunger was constitutional with him,
> women, cigarettes, liquor, need need need
> until he went to pieces.
> The pieces sat up & wrote. They did not heed
> their piecedom . . .

Berryman's poetic preferences and prejudices were definitely East Coast; although Oklahoma-born, he was proud of his trajectory from Columbia University to Clare College, Cambridge. So I soft-pedalled any references to my California friends, recalling the hostility I had witnessed between the palefaces, with their leafy New England campuses and professorial tweeds, and the redskins, with their New Directions and City Lights. If even Robert Creeley, who had been to Harvard (that other Cambridge), always provoked a snarl, there was no point in my mentioning Robert Duncan, although he and Berryman seemed, in their different ways, among the most learned poets I had met. Ironically, despite Berryman's preference for the genteel East Coast over the Wild West, he often resembled nothing so much as a rough cowboy from some old Western. Grizzled, cantankerous, tough-talking and hard-drinking, he could look like a kind of bardic Gaby Hayes.

And he could be wildly funny as he discussed what one should do about hostile critics: the Chinese torture of a thousand cuts was suggested, or roasting them alive slowly. Since several prominent modern critics would be involved in these hilarious midnight discussions, I will give no names, recalling only the solemnity with which he passed over one on whom we had disagreed: 'He's yours, John, of course', continuing with sombre gallantry, 'Please feel free to decide the punishment. Stocks, whips, or rack.' We both agreed that the critics we most admired were real writers themselves, from Ben Jonson to Doctor Johnson, from Coleridge to Eliot, but there were always problems with close contemporaries. Berryman confessed that he was so upset by Robert Lowell's grudging review of *77 Dream Songs* that the praise of the regular-army critics could not console him. We diagnosed competitive envy: 'Cal always wanted to be Number One.' Writers as critics were by definition programmatic, tangled in sibling rivalries, but at least we knew what was happening on the nursery floor. On the other hand, if one was going to set up as a professional critic, perhaps one should do like the psychoanalysts, and undergo scrutiny oneself before being allowed to practise on others. Professional critics were usually more lopsided than poets, trying to work out their personal grudges and problems through a seemingly impersonal agenda.

But the deeper concerns were always there: Berryman was obsessed by the last poems of Yeats, the only book he had brought with him. So Ireland and Yeats were no accidental choice. Had he not written: 'I began work in verse-making as a burning, trivial disciple of the great Irish poet, William Butler Yeats'? 'Cuchulain Comforted' specifically haunted him, since he had wrought himself into a state of near-ecstasy through the persona of Henry. 'What does he mean, Montague?' he would ask urgently, before throwing back his head to intone, in transatlantic imitation of Yeats' Sligo chant: 'They sang, but had not human tunes nor words,/ Though all was done in common as before;/ They had changed their throats and had the throats of birds.'

To celebrate his sojourn and the completion of the *Dream Songs*, I tried to arrange a reading for Berryman at UCD. But all they could offer was the ritual five pounds for a performance, which seemed to me not merely ungenerous but ridiculous. Instead I hired a hall and, with the help of Liam Miller and Basil Payne, made sure that it would be filled. For the programme, Berryman had given me his lovely paean to Yeats:

> I have moved to Dublin to have it out with you,
> majestic Shade, You whom I read so well
> so many years ago . . .

But rumours began to filter in that he was fortifying himself for his first and last public appearance in Dublin; indeed, that he might let some pub swallow him up and not appear at all. But appear he did, lurching in late, and so began one of the strangest poetry readings I have ever been involved in. With great difficulty, Patrick Kavanagh had been persuaded to come, on the condition that the name of a certain Irish publisher was not pronounced. Kavanagh lurked in the back with his McDaids troop, coughing as he waited, while I tried to create the right atmosphere with an introduction, in which I said that this was the most important occasion of its kind since Robert Frost had read at UCD. Unfortunately I also mentioned my first meeting with Berryman in Iowa, which provoked protests from our distinguished guest, who disliked any mention of that state, which he regarded as a minor region of hell.

As I was weaving to the close of my warm-up, Berryman deserted the platform and began to greet old friends in the audience, like the composer Brian Boydell, whom he had known at Cambridge. The sight of Berryman enthusiastically embracing the great-domed Boydell fascinated our audience, and meant that I could proceed to the end of my peroration without further interruption. But when Berryman was wooed back to the platform, he began his reading graciously, thanking those responsible for the recent recognition of Irish poetry abroad, in particular the man whose name Mr Kavanagh did not wish to hear, Liam Miller of the Dolmen Press, who had printed our programme with Berryman's Yeats poem, but also the text of Kavanagh's television *Self-Portrait*, the design of which had displeased the Irish master.

Uproar, and exit Kavanagh, whose bulk and belligerence could make any entrance or exit a dramatic event, with great scuffling and snorting as that particular lion shuffled off. But many of his drinking pals remained, including one, the critic John Jordan, who could not restrain his mutterings of admiration for Berryman's more intense poems, when a line or word would strike him: he was nearly as drunk as the reader. Another unexpected but loyal supporter, Ronnie Drew of the Dubliners, an old Majestic drinking pal of Berryman, took exception to such unprofessional intrusions, and kept admonishing the critic in his gravelly rasp: 'Shut up, John!' Since the genial offender bore the same first name as Berryman and myself, John Berryman kept glancing up in a puzzled way, and once stopped short to look over at me. I tried to reassure him that it was another John – John Jordan – who was creating the inadvertent side show. Yet Berryman, not so much drunk as splendidly oblivious, did not seem to mind, and soon himself, Jordan and the audience in general were talking away as if he were reciting in Slattery's, as he so often did during his Dublin stay. 'Do you really like that poem?' he asked, after one listener had insisted that he re-read the terrifying poem on his father's suicide, which he had shown me only a week before:

> I stand above my father's grave with rage,
> often, often before
> I've made this awful pilgrimage . . .
>
> O ho alas alas
> When will indifference come, I moan & rave
> I'd like to scrabble till I got right down
> away down under the grass
>
> and ax the casket open to see
> just how he's taking it . . .

It was a roaring success, although a nerve-racking one, the apotheosis of Berryman's Dublin year.

His great Spanish briefcase was bulging with *Dream Songs*, good, bad and indifferent. (There was a series, for example, on the English mariner Sir Francis Chichester, whose perilous, solo voyage around the world somehow became identified with the poet's psychic buffetings. One *Dream Song* was meant to be handed to Sir Francis on his triumphant arrival home.) The sorting would come later; now he would relax a little before travelling on the Continent. Surveying their bulk, I marvelled at his one-hundred-and-eighty-degree swings between abandon and control.

In his youth he might have loved the noble rhetoric of Yeats, but his own magnum opus, the *Dream Songs*, was more like a drunken version of that sprawling masterpiece by a poet closer to his home, *Leaves of Grass*. In racing parlance, he was by Yeats out of Whitman, and as a Brooklyn-born Irishman, I also felt like a child of both those Great White Fathers. My friend Tom Parkinson describes how Yeats' *Collected Poems* fulfils his dream of the Sacred Book, where individual lyrics weave into the one radiant vision. But Whitman had already accomplished that through his overarching world view in *Leaves of Grass*. Gary Snyder's exfoliating scroll, Ginsberg's exhortations in *The Fall of America* and Duncan's *Passages* all emerged from Whitman's 'barbaric yawp', though mediated through Ezra Pound and William Carlos Williams. And despite Berryman's hostility to the New Poetics, and his summoning of the 'majestic shade,' it seemed to me that his true ancestor was also Walt Whitman: indeed, he had grown to look like 'the good grey poet.' And it had occurred to me that the *Dream Songs* were a series of Whitmanian arias crisscrossed with the discipline of an Elizabethan sonnet sequence.

A final glimpse of Berryman's extraordinary Irish stay. I had arranged to bring him into the Dublin hills to meet Garech Browne, hoping to record John for Claddagh Records. It was a glorious excursion, one of those May days that make Ireland seem paradisiacal, a pet of a day. Anthony Kerrigan, translator of Borges and Neruda, drove us up in his battered Mercedes, and we sat in the garden at Woodtown Manor, laughing and drinking under the stare of the strange, squat stone lion that the previous owner, the American painter Morris Graves, had rescued from some ruined house. Berryman spoke a lot about Robert Lowell, who would later marry Garech's great-eyed cousin, the writer Caroline Blackwood.

Then a small incident occurred which showed John's essential innocence. John Hurt had joined us after a hard day filming the swashbuckling *Sinful Davy* with John Huston in the Wicklow hills. He complained that his bottom was sore because the exacting director had refused to be satisfied by his fall from a horse, and insisted that he tumble again and again. When he saw Hurt, Berryman went silent. After a while he nudged me. 'That's John Hurt,' he whispered incredulously. I agreed, and went to get Hurt a glass. But Berryman was still agog as any schoolboy; he and his young wife, Kate, had seen *A Man for All Seasons* only a few days before. 'But how can he be here?' hissed Berryman. 'He's really famous; he's a star.' Later, when he was warmed up but before he had begun to list to starboard, Berryman started to recite and roar his *Dream Songs*, and Hurt unwittingly returned the compliment. He had never heard of John Berryman, but he was sure of what he heard that afternoon, as Berryman dipped and dived through falsetto, innuendo, jive talk, blackface coonery, all the startling range of his new work. 'Huffy Henry, Mr Heartbreak: the New Man,/ come to farm a crazy land . . . '. 'That man has genius,' observed Hurt, listening in astonishment. 'And it's burning him up,' he added prophetically.

Now that his job was done, Berryman seemed to be drinking at random. There was a silver tray on the lawn, laden with bottles, but instead of keeping to one type of drink, he just poured whatever was nearest him into his glass: whiskey, gin, vodka, white wine – an impossible mixture. In all my experience of Dublin drunks, and even the alcoholics of forlorn Fintona, I had never seen the like. It seemed an aberration of America's 'martini culture'. I had grown used, in American bars, to the glamour of the cocktail shaker, the tapering glasses garnished with olives or fruit, a legacy from pre-war nightclubs. But it was spirits the whole time, hardly ever wine or beer, even with a meal; yet Berryman's indiscriminate drinking of mostly hard liquor, in any and all combinations, was wilder than anything I had seen from Berkeley to Iowa to New York. Kate did not seem to know how to deal with the situation; when we finally carted him home, she confessed that she was not sure she would be able to hold out much longer. She opened the medicine cupboard to show phalanxes of pills: uppers, downers and everything in between.

Some time later, he called on us in Paris with his wife and daughter, bearded to the eyebrows like an American Moses. In fact, his appearance created quite a stir amongst our neighbours, who associated such luxuriant hirsuteness with *clochard*s rather than kings. It was a more subdued evening, but again Berryman paid no attention to what he was drinking, as long as it was alcoholic. His little daughter sat on his knee and laughed and pulled his beard. But when I said wistfully to Madeleine afterwards, 'Wasn't that sweet to see, father and daughter so loving?' Madeleine's reaction was classically swift and French. 'She had better enjoy him now,' she said grimly. 'She won't have him long.'

A tense, bespectacled intellectual against the background of a draughty Nissen hut in Iowa, a shaggy benevolent prophet holding forth in Jack Ryan's pub; those were the two opposing faces of John Berryman for me, as though, under the pressure of experience, he had followed Yeats' prescription and found his own opposite. But there was a final face, or absence, after the conflagration of achievement. When I was reading at the University of Minnesota, I called to see him. He was drying out in a local hospital, the famous Golden Valley which Saul Bellow describes in his preface to *Recovery*. He shuffled out of an Alcoholics Anonymous session, hands twitching, face pallid and uneasy as he greeted me. We talked for a while in his room while he squatted on his tatami, but there was little heart to it. The contrast with our previous meetings in Dublin, where he would thunder forth his latest *Dream Songs*, lovely or awful or 'dee-lish-ious' (his own phrase for praise) was too abrupt. He had recognised his alcoholism now, and was fighting valiantly against it, although he was ill at ease in such a constrained atmosphere. For not only his habits but his habits of work were linked with drink. The ramshackle structure of the *Dream Songs* is based as much upon the soarings and plunges of the chronic drunk as anything else: the longueurs and sudden revelations, the licence to both bore and blaze before an audience, all of which are part of any long day's journey into night.

Dublin, Round Two

Second time round, I decided to stay with Garech Browne at Woodtown Manor, hoping to work in peaceful isolation, with Mount Venus and the Hellfire Club behind, and the lights of Dublin glimmering below. If I had to resign myself to being largely alone, it might as well be in a marvellous setting. And as well as my own work, I hoped to collaborate with Garech on Claddagh; indeed, some of our best records date from that period. Hugh MacDiarmid came over to record *A Drunk Man Looks at the Thistle*, which I consider one of the best long poems of the twentieth century: the septagenerian Scot read straight through with hardly a stop. And with the help of the Scottish Arts Council, we began a series of recordings of other Scottish poets, which, of course, necessitated pleasant jaunts to Edinburgh, where much good whisky was consumed in the many Scottish equivalents of McDaids.

Yet Garech's private life was also in some turmoil, so that he was often away, and I would find myself alone in that luxurious but empty and echoing Georgian house. I suppose I was trying to cast Garech as my patron, but he refused to sit still long enough to fulfil the social obligations of that nurturing role. I was handsomely looked after by a skeleton staff, one of the last butlers in Ireland, and his wife the cook, but I often dined alone while Garech roamed, seeking to solve his romantic problems, and returning only occasionally, to supervise the production of another fine record, before bolting again.

So, while I was better housed and fed than in the shambling attic rooms of Anglesea Street, I was once again restive and lonely. So much so that I tried to teach myself to master a penny-farthing bicycle which Garech had recently bought and then abandoned. It was easy enough to clamber on, using the garden wall as a fillip, but almost impossible to get down from the high seat under the giant front wheel, except by barrelling into a tree or hedge. I gave up the pursuit of this antique skill when the bruises began to outnumber the pleasures. Then one evening while I was at the dining table, and perhaps looking wistful, the butler filled my glass and offered me some discreet advice: 'You shouldn't be on your own so much. You ought to be enjoying yourself more while you're still young.'

It had occurred to me during my long evenings alone that I could have been frequenting the company of colleagues, stopping with fellow lecturers for a pre-prandial pint, or, indeed, dining with them in a restaurant or at home with their wives or husbands. The problem was that the academics I had come to know did not seem to recognise how forlornly footloose I was. I believe that the Dublin of that period was still an old-fashioned city of closely woven families. In other words, someone living alone in a flat or a friend's house, without relations to succour him, was a foreign notion to most of my colleagues. Or else I was living too far out, or perhaps they were chary of too much social contact with fellow lecturers. Anyway, I was seldom, if ever, invited to the homes of those I greeted in the corridors of the university. I suppose they could not have known how appealing a family evening would have been to this virtual bachelor.

That spring term, I was conducting a seminar on modern Irish poetry for Roger McHugh and the Anglo-Irish literature course, but I was also saddled with a lengthy series of unexpected lectures on the eighteenth century, which I hoped would bring me back to my deferred thesis on Oliver Goldsmith. At the same time, Garech had developed a new enthusiasm for antique coaches. And as preparation for my lectures on the eighteenth century, I would try to conjure up the atmosphere of that period by accompanying him to local hostelries in one or other of his ornate carriages, whenever he was in residence. Garech drove in a coachman's hat and cape, flourishing his long whip, while several ladies giggled inside. One of these was a young Californian who had turned up in the Bailey and was cutting a swathe through literary Dublin.

An exchange student at TCD, she had a milk-white complexion, and long black hair inherited from her Crow grandmother. That glossy hair falling in panels on either side of her large-eyed face, along with her miniskirts and flat shoes, gave her the innocent look popular at that time. Yet, also in keeping with the times, she was sexually adventurous; whether this was because of her own impulses or because she believed that erotic abandon was expected of her, I did not know. At any rate, I had been warned against her charms, because the locals were astonished by such transatlantic sexual boldness, but I was vulnerable, and her flower-child freedom, so exotic in Dublin, recalled Berkeley and appealed to my loneliness. Once more I had found myself, though married, living like a bachelor, so why not have some of the obvious consolations? Therefore I stopped trying to resist, and took the butler's advice. Yet I was tempting fate, and knew it.

Even more important, I was growing increasingly unhappy with the declining state of UCD as it prepared to flit to Belfield. I was of the Donogh O'Malley faction – the Minister for Education who argued for a great city university in the heart of town, with UCD to balance and complement the mellow Georgian presence of Trinity. It seemed to me that the Iveagh Gardens, where generations of students had strolled and courted; 86 St Stephens Green, where a lonely Gerard Manley Hopkins had prayed in his simple room overlooking the Dublin hills and had written his *Terrible Sonnets*; and Newman's little jewel of a church together constituted a rich heritage that should not be squandered. Had it not already helped produce the Father of Authors, our great exemplar, James Joyce?

During my own university years, our reactionary president Michael Tierney, who loathed the influence of Joyce, had given me my first experience of censorship when he banned an issue of the *National Student* in which, ironically, there was a poem of mine about the temptation to Celtic sanctity. Tierney seemed a monster, and if I were Dante, I would have banished him to a special suburban hell barren of beauty and full of concrete buildings. He was supported in his campaign to uproot UCD from the city centre by Jeremiah Joseph Hogan, our former English professor, who had bored us all with his electroplated Oxford accent as he droned the same stilted lectures from the same yellowing pages year after year, or intoned from the set text, usually yards of Milton, halting to declare with great solemnity: 'There are some fine things here.' (That is, if we were unlucky enough to hear him: half the time a belated note would be pinned up by the beloved college porter, stating in big letters: PROFESSOR HOGAN WILL NOT LECTURE TODAY DUE TO THE INDISPOSITION OF A SORE THROAT.)

So Tierney was a boor, who ran roughshod over students, while Hogan was a bore. Between them they tried to hijack whatever burgeoning tradition UCD might have had. It was, of course, a right-wing Catholic conspiracy, intended to save the souls of future Catholic scholars by isolating them before they could be seduced by false gods, like thinking, feeling, loving and living for oneself or, God forbid, following the examples of those great Catholic writers who had been associated with the institution in its infancy. It was a cliché in Dublin that UCD was a Fine Gael university, and that Tierney had been the intellectual mentor of the Blueshirts. Some of my early professors, like John Marcus O'Sullivan, were directly connected with the first, conservative Cosgrave government, while the Philosophy Department was dominated by that latter-day Savonarola, Canon Horgan, who had more than the ear of the Archbishop of Dublin. This ethos seemed to rub off on some of my colleagues, like the Law professor, John Kelly. Even some of my older colleagues in the English Department did not seem immune from such doctrinaire Catholic conservatism.

Ironically, as that transplantation was taking place, some of the major buildings encircling Earlsfort Terrace were coming up for sale, including Alexandra College, the most famous Protestant girls' school in Ireland. (How often had we gazed yearningly across at those alien figures of young Protestant womanhood, swinging their satchels as they sauntered to and from classes.) And Todd Andrews was about to make the biggest mistake of his career, in closing down the Harcourt Street railway line, which had served south Dublin for so long. Harcourt Street Station was an august Georgian building of Portland stone, which would have made a splendid addition to UCD as well. Coincidence, synchronicity, call it what you will. The facts were plain: just as UCD needed more space, Dublin was making it possible for the university to unfurl within the city itself, by releasing lovely old buildings as if by magic. But the Blueshirt reactionary brigade refused to read the signs and, instead, transplanted UCD to a sterile suburban campus more evocative of an American prairie college than a great European university.

PART III

4

CLADDAGH GOES NORTH

OR THE NORTHERN MUSE

The North of Ireland from which I emerged was barely comprehensible to my Southern contemporaries. In the 1950s, a threadbare, post-Emergency Dublin was grappling with poverty, priests and politics, and had little time or inclination to consider the complexities of the North. This obliviousness lingered well into the sixties. The fiery Bernadette Devlin, that modern-day Joan of Arc, would not impress herself on the outside world until late in the decade. As for poetry, it is hard now, after the advent of poets like Seamus Heaney, Derek Mahon, Michael Longley, Medbh McGuckian, Ciaran Carson and Paul Muldoon, to imagine a Northern Ireland that was not a literary hotbed. But I was regarded not as one of the first of a new movement, but as an anomaly: I had no poetic contemporaries from the North. Although Tom Kinsella accepted an offer to become one of the directors of Mary O'Malley's Lyric Theatre in Belfast, he was suspicious of any of the survivors of the wartime crusade towards Ulster regionalism, which had been fostered by John Hewitt and others. And when I made reference to my Northern origins, he would counter, with a gruff laugh: 'You're not like them. You had the good sense to come down here.'

The urban north-east was more or less foreign to me, since

I had not gone to Queen's University. In the fifties and sixties I would befriend two older poets of Protestant background, John Hewitt and Louis MacNeice, who were both from that remote north-east, but Dublin had become my source. And yet, again and again, I was drawn to make pilgrimages northwards to my own old home west of the River Bann, in County Tyrone. After all, the place where one is brought up haunts the mind and heart, and furthermore I was well into my long, complicated poem on my complicated home territory, *The Rough Field*.

I was always trying to persuade my friend and fellow director (indeed the founding father) of Claddagh Records, Garech Browne, to consider the literary and musical possibilities of our lost Six Counties. But like most of my Dublin pals, Garech doubted that the stern North could yield much fruit. Yet he had met some musical eccentrics from Ulster at the various *fleadhs cheoil*, like Dr Galligan from Cavan ('an atrocious tin-whistle player,' according to the discerning Garech), who dressed as colourfully as any Irish-American on parade. But he was chairman of Comhaltas, the All-Ireland Traditional Music Association. And there was Brian O'Donnell, a squat, saturnine man, and a direct descendant of the great Donegal family, who was head of the Belfast branch of the Comhaltas. These two were prodigious drinkers, yet, on the other hand, in the middle of the flowing *fleadhs*, you might catch the honeyed tones of Paddy Tunney from Fermanagh, a practising Pioneer, or Temperance man, whom I first heard singing the original Sligo version of 'She Moved Through the Fair.'

And then there was David Hammond, that soft-eyed, sweet-voiced singer from Belfast, a close pal of Seamus Heaney (whose wife Marie sang beautifully – though only late at night, with friends). Of course there was also Seamus himself, who was beginning to be known both for his early books of poetry and as part of an embryonic literary movement in Belfast, which

arech Browne, heir of the Guinness Brewing Co. and co-founder of Claddagh Records, stands before a ortrait of himself painted by Lucien Freud, grandson of Sigmund Freud.

(© Alen MacWeeney/CORBIS)

Poet Robert Graves

Philosopher and writer Jean-Paul Sartre with his partner, writer and intellectual Simone de Beauvoir
(© Georges Pierre/Sygma/Corbi

llen Ginsberg (photographed by Gary Snyder) during an eight-day backpack climbing trip in a wilder-
ess area of Northern Cascades National Park, Washington State, in the summer of 1965

Poet John Berryman, May 1967

Poet Robert Bly

Beat poet Gary Snyder in a restaurant in Kyoto, Japan. The photograph was taken by Allen Ginsberg when the two men met up before a poetry conference in Vancouver, British Columbia.

Poet Robert Creeley

Engraver and painter Bill Hayter ('a lean, wiry Englishman')
and Desiree Moorehead ('a genuine Irish beauty')

Future Taoiseach Charles Haughey:
'those shrewd, narrowed eyes; that blunt face,
like a hammer-headed shark'

'Sixties icon' Abbie Hoffman at the opening of the People's Flag Show, Judson Memorial Church, Washington Square, New York, 9 November 1970

(© Jan Van Raay)

Patrick Kavanagh
(*Illustrated London News*, 9 December 1967,
© The Illustrated London News Picture
Library, London/The Bridgeman Art Library)

Student leader Mario Savio, *c.* 1964–65
(*San Francisco News-Call Bulletin* Newspaper Photograph Archive, Free Speech Movement Selection)

had spilled over into the Belfast Festival and was finally catching the attention of the South. Seamus had read at the Lantern Theatre in Dublin during our reading series, his first public reading in that city. And in due course I was invited to Queen's University Belfast, and took that opportunity to try to indoctrinate my reluctant friend, Garech, into Northern ways of poetry and traditional music.

Garech had been to Tyrone with me before, in friendship, on voyages of mercy. When my beloved Aunt Brigid was taken to Omagh Hospital, he drove me up to see her. Looking with exhausted, rheumy eyes at my long-haired friend, she clasped my hand and murmured: 'Who is that lady with you?' And when my Aunt Mary lay dying in the Tyrone farmhouse where she had been born, Garech once again drove me to the deathbed. But this was to be a business journey; I would read, and then Garech and I would explore Belfast's musical and literary possibilities, for future records.

It was a principle of my honourable friend that one should always do things in style. So the big motor car had to be polished before we set out on his maiden voyage to alien Belfast. (I think he had been close to Belfast once, in Downpatrick, to see his half-brother Gay Kindersley, the famous amateur jockey, risk his neck in the steeplechase. But he would have been cocooned in his mother's chauffeur-driven Rolls-Royce. And he might also have gone in style to Clandeboye to visit his relations there, including the distinguished novelist Caroline Blackwood.) This time, I tried to interest Garech in the historical nature of our journey, insisting that we halt to see the three lovely High Crosses at Monasterboice, one of the great sites of the early Irish Church, and of course the dark drama of the Gap of the North, the landscape of the Great Táin, where Cuchulainn held the pass against the armies of Queen Medbh of Connacht, Garech's home province. But my learned commentary was cut

129

short when, nearing the border, both I and the car ran out of what the Americans call 'gas'. There we sat, a seething poetic Ratty and a tow-headed Mr Toad, stalled in his big idle automobile, five minutes from the border, under the holy mountain of Slieve Gullion. I was due to give my first reading in Queen's in a few short hours, and we had not put on the nosebag, nor had I yet wet my whistle – a few modest scoops being an indispensable pre-reading ritual, of course.

While I fumed, Garech fussed about in the boot, before triumphantly producing a small petrol tin. Then off he toddled towards the nearest petrol station, just south of the border, because petrol happened to be cheaper there at that time. So we were soon on the road again, myself still trembling with hunger, thirst and exasperation, all intensified by pre-reading nerves. Garech knew full well that he was endangering the evening by his negligence, but he was also aware of his friend's – and indeed his own – needs. 'Perhaps we should have a little pit stop?' he murmured diplomatically. 'I'm sure you remember that lovely man, Frank Sweeney the chemist, whom we met at the *fleadh* in Boyle. Doesn't he live in a place called Daisy Hill, in Newry?'

I did know Frank Sweeney, an engaging fellow, like all the Sweeneys, but even madder than most of that mad tribe, who had been cursed in olden times for defying an officious cleric. Since then, one Sweeney in each family seems to be afflicted with a terrible restlessness. Frank's version of this ancient curse was that, although he was a splendid fiddler, he could never end a tune, but would swerve abruptly off into another one. This would startle his fellow players, who thought they were taking part in a friendly session, and would look forward to finishing an air with a fine flourish, only to be compelled to plunge into something else before they knew what was happening.

Mrs Sweeney attended us because Frank was ill, convalescing after a heart attack that had brought him to Daisy Hill Hospital.

She sat us down by the fire, with thick ham sandwiches and large glasses of whiskey, while Frank told us about his travails. It seemed that he had nearly wrecked the morale of the hospital by refusing, in true Sweeney fashion, to stay in his bed after the operation. He had also concealed four fiddles somewhere in the hospital, which he played day and night, until the nurses confiscated them one by one. He declared that he was now in fine fettle, and ready for any fun, but Mrs Sweeney was clearly not too keen on the idea of him travelling on with us to Belfast, even for a night of mind-improving poetry.

We made it, of course, as one usually does, surmounting the obstacles, and I had my first indication of the new feeling that was unfurling in Belfast, dead capital of my Northern youth. An excitement crackled in the air around the reading, not necessarily generated by my performance; there was simply an energy that I had not before experienced in that rather dour city. And afterwards, a warm band of the faithful moved to the Ulster Arts Club, which was then in Wellington Road. Our Belfast guides, Heaney and Hammond, seemed to know it well, and relished the excuse the poetry reading gave for an after-hours libation. Garech surmised that they loved the club because Belfast seemed to offer few other distractions. A low-church town, it maintained strict licensing hours in the pubs, and there was a dearth of restaurants. So the Arts Club, Garech concluded as we ascended the stairs, was probably pretty much 'it' as far as Belfast social life was concerned. And sure enough, when we entered, we were greeted by a coven of actors, led by J. G. Devlin, whose rasping voice welcomed us warmly.

It was a famous night, like many famous future nights in Belfast, and afterwards Garech and I kipped together in the newly married Heaneys' first house. I had never slept with Garech before, and would be reluctant to do so again, because his headful of rough hair was as prickly as a haystack or a mountain ram, tickling my nose or ears whenever I tried to settle down to sleep.

In the morning, we dragged ourselves to the Arts Council of Northern Ireland, where we discussed possible projects with the Director, Ken Jamieson. My own priorities were simple: to try and get a little money to end *The Rough Field*, and to organise a series of poetry records, similar to our Kavanagh and Beckett efforts, but focusing on the North this time. Our series of Scottish poets had been supported by the Arts Council of Scotland, and we were hopeful for a similar arrangement with the Arts Council of Northern Ireland. In the choice of music, I had to defer to Garech, whose long-standing prejudice against some Northern traditional music, which he considered impure, I was trying to topple.

This attempt led to further Northern visits, which were often hilarious. We went to see my old Irish schoolmaster, Seán O'Boyle, in Armagh, in order to give Garech a dose of the deep, hill-enfolded South Armagh tradition, one of the oldest areas of Ireland, the Ulster equivalent of the Black Hills of South Dakota. Seán and Garech got on very well, with Seán murmuring over the Bushmills about the connection between the 'old stock' of the west of Ireland and traditional music, as in the days of the harper Carolan. This frustrated me a bit, because, in keeping with my campaign, I would have liked Seán to extol the North, especially since he had edited a collection of Ulster songs in Irish. But Seán had begun to spend his spare time in the Connemara Gaeltacht, and was waxing enthusiastic about Garech's home country instead. This did have a good outcome: Garech was able to enlist him to write sleeve notes for some of our forthcoming records of *sean nos*. But their new friendship did not help to foster records celebrating Northern music, and Garech did not help by referring to a fiddler from Belfast, Seán Maguire, who was famous for his old-fashioned, plangent, café style, as 'that Northern fucker'. We were in a hotel in The Moy, an elegant eighteenth-century town, near the birthplace of Paul Muldoon, who had also been taught Irish by Seán O'Boyle. The locals, who adored Maguire, would have lynched Garech for his blasphemy, if I had not pleaded, in my most dulcet Northern tones, for tolerance of this ignorant west-of-Ireland man.

We survived, only to try again, using the legendary Brian O'Donnell as our guide this time: he had just been hosting a Spanish O'Donnell in his little red-brick Belfast house. I placed my trust in O'Donnell because, besides being the local head of Comalhtas, he was an advisor on Irish music for BBC Northern Ireland. He was a swarthy, nearly simian man, with the tough energy peculiar to that sturdy type, even if the only exercise he seemed to perform was lofting glasses. Often after some inter-view or poetry reading for the local radio or television, I would find him lying in wait to spirit me away to either the 'hospitality room' or else the nearest hostelry. But this time he did introduce us to the local folk club, where we heard some music other than the clink of glasses. And Garech re-met an old *fleadh* acquain-tance, an RUC man, ironically called Detective Browne. He was mad about Irish music, but his occupation prevented him from being a member of any Irish organisation, even if it was not political but purely cultural or musical. Both sides would natural-ly have disapproved: the RUC smelling disloyalty, Comhaltas fearing a spy. Garech, a Protestant eccentric himself, was fasci-nated by the man's plight, and also considered him a good accor-dion player.

It was the weekend, and Brian kept mumbling that the best music was to be heard 'up the country', in the Glens of Antrim, evoking memories of Roger Casement and *feiseanna*. So, late on a Sunday morning, we sailed up the Coast Road, beyond Carrickfergus, in search of traditional music. It was a lovely day, but I began to wonder why, as we came to each small village,

Brian would briefly disappear, muttering darkly about his 'mission' before summoning us, with a crooked finger, into some dark snug or forlorn hotel bar. We gathered that all the musicians had fled to the hills, or fallen by the wayside, but there were rumours of a great session assembling in a place called The Blue Pool, in Glengarriff. By late afternoon we did reach The Blue Pool, yet another, larger, hotel bar, with not a note of music in it, only the usual furtive Sunday drunks, slumping at the counter, and the usual dank stoor of carpets and Guinness. Heads lifted from pint glasses to greet Brian like a long-lost friend, and then Garech and I realised that we had fallen victim to the cruel licensing laws of the North. In other words, Brian had all along been questing not for the lovely airs of Antrim, but for the ultimate Sabbath watering hole.

I think it was early that same Sunday morning that Garech and I were waiting for Brian near Carlisle Circle on the border of north Belfast. We observed men hurrying out from the side streets, many carrying musical instruments, fifes and pipes, and little plastic bags from which they exhumed the pressed glory of the broad orange sashes their fathers wore. It was obviously a warm-up for the Twelfth of July, a cultural event with which Garech was certainly unfamiliar. And, indeed, we soon heard the rumble of approaching bands, the brattle of Lambeg drums and the shrilling of the fife. A crowd was gathering to watch this parade rehearsal, so that presently we found ourselves in the middle of a crush of mostly men, with a scattering of hushed children. I tried to make myself look as subdued, sober and almost Protestant as possible, as the bands began marching sturdily past, often with service medals clanking on their serge-clothed breasts beneath those sombre bowler hats. To my dismay, my friend proceeded to make seemingly guileless observations in his clarion, upper-class voice, oblivious to the tensions surrounding this display of pomp. 'They look a bit like an army of Laurel and Hardys, yes?' he said amusedly. 'But I do think that some of the music is rather interesting. Didn't James Galway play the flute in one of these bands?'

I had become uneasily aware that our presence was being noticed. With his classic Aran gansey roped by a lovely Aran crios, or embroidered sash, and his long Cavalier hair bound by a velvet ribbon, Garech would have stood out in any company. But he was a glowing contrast to this Roundhead crowd, a lat-ter-day Lord Ashbourne, a Protestant aristocrat who had insist-ed on speaking Gaelic and sporting a saffron kilt – to the embar-rassment of his neighbours.

We were under particular scrutiny from a lean man with a blanched face and very light hair (nearly an albino), who was bristling with a kind of hostile energy. Finally he positioned him-self between me and Garech, and launched into an Ulster ver-sion of the third degree, to determine our true-blue credentials.

'You see them men there? Them's fine men. Look at the medals bouncing on their chests.'

Both Garech and I were silent, although Garech, still fascinated by the blend of fife and flute, appeared to sense no menace.

'Them men have served their country. Them men is Queen's men.'

Garech, still unperturbed, gave him a vague smile, complete-ly unaware of the audience we were gathering.

'Aye, them's Queen's men. D'you see that big building up there? That's a prison, Crumlin Road Jail. And there's men in there now, for serving the Queen. And d'you know, I'd be glad to serve her any time, to get rid of some of that Catholic vermin.'

I think he was referring to 'Gusty' Spence, who had been condemned for sectarian violence but who, ironically, would become an eloquent crusader for peace in the North. But having been caught in somewhat similar circumstances before, in my native Tyrone, I was aware of the potential for a blow-up. (Recently, travelling from Derry to Belfast by train after a reading at Magee College, I had been cornered by two fairly attractive, quite genteel Protestant ladies. They proceeded to inform me how badly things were going in the North. 'The Tagues are getting out of hand again,' they said bitterly. 'We'll have to put manners on them.' They were quite unaware that this tall man, wearing a long French coat and stylish boots, was himself a Tague in drag, a *Mon*-tague. As I would come to write: 'My own name/ Hatred's synonym.')

Garech, by this time, had realised that we were encircled by suspicion. With wide, candid eyes, he regarded our interlocutor and inquired, in his most polite drawing-room tones: 'The Queen? Do you know her?'

The pallid man gawped, his mouth falling open. I had forgotten that Garech's complicated lineage included a droplet of Stuart blood. (He is descended from Mary, Queen of Scots through that swarthy, pleasure-loving king Charles II, and his Breton Catholic mistress, Louise de Cernaouille.) And he had described to me an awkward moment of protocol with Her Majesty at St James's Palace, when, while taking his leave, he had stepped backwards, to collide with the Queen Mother's bum. (Of course, as a Stuart whose ghostly ancestors were Charles I, Charles II and Bonny Prince Charlie, he could not completely acknowledge the Hanover woman, except as a Teutonic usurper.) He did not reveal this to our Orange friend, however, but merely observed: 'I've met the Queen. I must say, I found our conversation a bit boring. John here says that she actually reads T. S. Eliot, but I did not find that we had much in common. What do you think of her?'

The man's mouth had reached his chin, as if he had been winded by what he had just heard. And the other onlookers, who might have expected some crude, Tague-baiting sport, moved back from us, leaving us in a kind of charmed circle. In the old days, people used to travel from remote parts of England to be cured of scrofula by the royal touch. Samuel Johnson was brought to Westminster as a boy for that purpose. And here was someone who had actually touched, or had been touched by, the mythic presence of their monarch. It was as if a Catholic had said, with an idle authority, that he had indeed seen the Blessed Virgin, and had conversed with her. I still do not know to what degree Garech understood the danger we might have been in; but I do know that his brilliantly supercilious tones rescued us that day. (When he heard this story, our musical Detective Browne assured us that, if matters had really got out of hand, the RUC would eventually have saved us, but we probably would have needed several days in hospital.)

We did in the end produce some splendid records by the singer Len Graham, and that cherubic harper from Belfast, Derek Bell, who would be enlisted into The Chieftains. And when Ciaran Carson, poet and musician, became traditional arts officer of the Arts Council of Northern Ireland, he gave us many suggestions for recording players, who were often from my own neighbouring county of Fermanagh. But Claddagh had begun to falter in a world where small record companies, like small publishers, were being gobbled up by corporations; industry moguls and accountants were now determining what would be produced. This would work well for The Chieftains, since their leader, Paddy Moloney, had a good business head, though their success meant that newer, younger groups began with great expectations, which modest Claddagh could not fulfil.

During the period when Michael Longley was literature officer of the Arts Council of Northern Ireland, however, I managed to get a small bursary to complete *The Rough Field*. And we began a series of recordings of poets from the North. The first, called 'The Northern Muse', featuring myself and Seamus Heaney, and the second, a solo album from Derek Mahon, were the first projects in which the Arts Councils of both the North and South participated. Longley was also organising poetry-reading tours around the North, featuring himself and Seamus, James Simmons and Paul Muldoon. And at a crucial time in the North's history, myself and my old friend John Hewitt embarked on a tour called 'The Planter and the Gael,' a poetic effort to improve community relations in our divided province.

5

The Planter and the Gael

or An Ulster Tandem

My first meeting with John Hewitt was not a success. Passing through Belfast on my way home to Tyrone, I paid the Ulster Museum a visit, and asked for the poet. A stocky, bespectacled, rather gruff man emerged from behind a glass door. (I may have been prompted to call because we had both had poems read out in an early poetry competition organised by Austin Clarke on Radio Éireann, prize three guineas each.) But he clearly did not know me from Adam. Also, I was timid and tongue-tied, and he made no effort to put me at my ease. We wandered silently through the gallery, where I grasped at a familiar straw by stopping before Sir John Lavery's portrait of Cardinal MacRory. 'He's my second cousin,' I ventured proudly. 'His mother's name is Montague.'

'It's a bad painting,' declared the unyielding Hewitt. We were both right, but his rebuke was brusque, if not brutal.

I knew his work already, from copies of *Lagan*, bulky as a train timetable, which I had unearthed in the dusty corner of a Derry bookshop. W. R. Rodgers was then the acclaimed Ulster poet, but I found Hewitt more to my taste, even the bigoted bits, like 'the Romish pit' in his poem 'The Glittering Sod'. To offset that, there was his shy visit to a Catholic church in 'The Lonely Heart':

The years since then have proved I should have stayed
and mercy might have touched me till I prayed.

It reminded me of my Protestant neighbours in Garvaghey, dour but friendly, coming awkwardly in to contribute a coin at the funeral offerings. (It was a dreadful 'Romish' practice of the period, because the priest would read aloud not only the names of the contributors, but the amount they had subscribed to honour the dead. In this alien atmosphere, the Protestants offered a token, a modest half-crown or so, which placed them amongst the parish poor. So the last names I heard as an altar boy would have been: 'Robert Clarke, half a crown; Albert McLean, half a crown; George Rainey, half a crown.')

But Hewitt's essay on 'some problems of the Ulster writer', called 'The Bitter Gourd', ruffled my west-of-the-Bann sensibility – along with its misuse of the term 'Ulster,' to describe only part of our fractured province. Yet clearly Hewitt was a thinking man – a little slow perhaps, but genuine. I was disappointed when this argument with himself, as Yeats would call it, was excluded from *No Rebel Word* (1948), his first main collection of poetry. The title seemed to suggest that he was a conservative in politics and language, alien to the Republic that had been brought about by the Easter Rebellion and even to the 1798 Rebellion in his own beloved Antrim and Belfast. But that title does not do justice to the careful complexity of his lonely thought.

We were brought back into touch when Mary O'Malley had the generous idea of installing John as poetry editor of *Threshold*, the literary magazine of Belfast's Lyric Theatre. By the time he had published some of my poems, including 'The Water Carrier', in the magazine, and saluted my first slim volume, *Forms of Exile* (1959), the austere figure I had met in the museum in Stranmillis had definitely mellowed. (The editors did, however, amend my story about boarding school, 'That Dark

Accomplice', replacing the word 'farted' with the more genteel 'belched'.) Slowly a working friendship was established because, meanwhile, in my small Paris studio, I was busy assembling the first serious study of Hewitt, which he gratefully described in museum terms as 'building up a hairy monster from a trickle of bones'. I had broken through that crusty exterior to uncover a profound loneliness. Writing from Coventry on my Poetry Ireland study of his work, 'Regionalism into Reconciliation', he said: 'I doubt if there's another mortal who has taken so much trouble to grasp its tendency.'

Passed over for promotion in the Ulster Museum where I had first met him, because, he said with a grim chuckle, of his association 'with Catholics and Communists', Hewitt had exiled himself to the Coventry Municipal Art Gallery. It was, in a way, a homecoming for the more English part of his psyche, and the rehabilitation of the city after the wartime bombings, with the new, very modern cathedral soaring from the ruins, appealed to his socialist side. He describes 'its famous steeples and its web of girders,/ as image of the state hope argued for . . . ' in his passionate poem 'An Irishman in Coventry'. (Note that he does not write 'Ulsterman' and even identifies with his old Catholic neighbours: 'the whiskey-tinctured breath, the pious buttons,/ called up a people endlessly betrayed/ by our own weakness . . .')

I called on his wife Roberta (or Ruby) and himself in Coventry several times. Stratford and Shakespeare were a touristic blur, but one afternoon he brought me round to see E. M. Forster, who was nearly ninety, and as frail as a moth. John, it seemed, had been reading to him regularly, including my poem 'The Trout', which the old man remembered as being 'very sensuous'. Imagine how I felt, as a still relatively young Irish poet, listening to a master of English prose quoting some of my own lines, particularly: 'As the curve of my hands/ Swung under his body/ He surged, with visible pleasure'. And I thought I was describing how to catch a fish!

Forster was staying in, and probably paying for, Big Bob Buckingham's house. Big Bob was a kind-hearted, burly former policeman, one of those sturdy, red-faced, official-looking English figures − like our postman when I was a child, Mr Blemings, whose shiny boots I had admired. I realised, of course, that this was the mythical love object who haunted Forster's later years, a male muse figure, and an image of Saxon virility, in contrast to Forster's own delicacy. How some of my homosexual poet friends in Dublin would have envied me meeting this legend, but it did not seem to me that there was anything physical between the two men, only Forster's burning admiration for Big Bob's 'fine manly form'. Because Mrs Bob was also there, bustling about and serving tea, like any decent, middle-class English wife. And Forster spoke of her with great warmth. It seemed that Big Bob had been quite sick, probably with a heart attack, and when he was taken to hospital, she made sure that their frail friend was kept informed of the fate of their mutual beloved. Morgan Forster's voice trembled with feeling as he recalled the ordeal.

John Hewitt and I did not discuss what we had seen in any detail. He seemed to have a kind of Protestant prudery: we never, for example, mentioned the childlessness which was a problem in both our marriages. Yet I carried away from that memorable afternoon a strong sense of John's unobtrusive care for his fellow man: he was dutiful, yes, but also tender and comprehending. Looking back from my bus seat the next day, I saw John, large-hatted as Ezra Pound, waving goodbye with his stick. He was beginning to accept with pride the senior poet's role, and I was glad to have played my part, persuading MacGibbon & Kee, my own publishers, to publish a (nearly) *Collected Poems*, although the selection still seemed to me a too-safe one, eschewing argument, and with too many poetic postcards from Greece, searching for solace. Still, John was glad, writing to me in October 1968: 'Publication of *C.P.* has meant a lot to me, coming at this time, a hope I had hugged against all apparent reason.'

Our first 'Planter and Gael' tour encompassed a week in late November 1970. We had already come together for a broadcast in the curving stone studios of BBC Northern Ireland in Belfast. John had travelled from Coventry, and I from Paris via Dublin. John was curt almost to the point of silence, still profoundly pessimistic about any possible effect poetry might have on our frozen North. 'I have no audience,' he kept repeating glumly, still in his Coventry cast of mind. 'Maybe we'll have one after this tour,' I offered, but he only shook his white head ruefully.

Nevertheless I think John and I, who were both living abroad, saw the tour not only as a return to our home territory but also as a half-serious, half-lighthearted attempt at community relations during an increasingly fraught time. And it worked very well, except that few if any Planters emerged from their fastnesses to hear us. On our first night in the Adair Arms Hotel in Ballymena, a tall, handsome blonde lady swept up to us, declaring 'I am Jane Chichester-Clarke' in a crisp, unmistakably English voice. 'We don't hear much poetry round here,' she continued with a dry smile. There was no sign of her MP husband Robin, however, or his brother James, who would become Prime Minister of the North of Ireland. And Big Ian Paisley had not bothered to come either, no doubt scorning our different form of oratory.

Though the Gaels took Hewitt to their heart, we gradually gave up all hope of meeting Prods or Planters – except in a formal context, like the New University of Ulster in Coleraine and the Portora Royal School in Enniskillen (alma mater of

Wilde and Beckett), where we were received with professional politeness. Only in the County Museum of Armagh did things become a little tense. Armagh was, after all, the scene of my own harsh schooling, and John and I walked those history-freighted streets and walls from our base in the Charlemont Arms Hotel, exchanging our different memories. He would have come down to Armagh from Belfast on museum business, to see John Luke, that curiously elegant painter, or the Presbyterian pastor poet W. R. Rodgers. Hewitt's people had come from Kilmore in the Armagh countryside, but he did not seem to have any especially intimate feeling for that little stone city, wound round its two cathedrals.

During the museum performance, in my commentary on my poem 'Clear the Way', I spoke about visiting my favourite place of worship in Armagh, the Chapel of the Royal Irish Fusiliers in the old Protestant cathedral, and of finding it empty, perhaps because so many of the families whose names were inscribed on the Roll of Honour would not feel at home there. In other words, the Roll was crowded with as many Tagues as Prods – there were O's and Macs galore – but their descendants doubtless felt that they could not venture easily into that fine sombre place. The heads of the two major churches were in the audience, and the Protestant Archbishop found my remark tactless. Indeed, I had intended it to provoke some thought about our brutal dichotomies, in which Ulstermen from both sides of the house were united only in death, on a foreign field.

In Omagh's Royal Arms Hotel, Kitty Horisk, the sweet wife of perhaps my oldest friend and first surrogate father, Barney, grasped my arm: 'Don't let us down the night, or I'll kill ye.' And afterwards, speaking of Hewitt: 'That man's no Planter. It's a rare breed of Protestant that speaks about "getting along".' (She was referring to John's allegorical poem, 'The Colony', in which he speaks of an effort to 'make common cause with the natives, in their hearts . . . '.) A relation of mine buzzed around, complaining that some of my books, a legacy from my mother's house, were blocking her garage door. Introduced to the placid, pipe-smoking Hewitt after our reading, she said sourly: 'I suppose you're selfish, like all poets.' (A conclusion that was hardly scientific, since I was the only example she'd met before then.)

John particularly enjoyed our insider's tour of Omagh, which he barely knew, despite its being a garrison town, dominated by a stern courthouse, towards which the whole town seemed to sweep. We walked through the streets at night, with old friends of myself and Ben Kiely, who gave us an insider's tour of the town. They spoke about corpulent Davy Young, the Protestant barber who had an addiction to practical jokes, and the strange story of Half-Hanged Norton, who survived the rope on Gallows Hill, where Kiely had grown up. There was talk, too, of pearl-fishing on the Strule, in glass-bottomed boats.

That first tour, so ably arranged by Michael Longley, had been such a success that we were asked to undertake another, the following spring. But even in that short time, the mood in the North had changed, hardened by bitter experience on both sides. Some of this had been charted by John in his pamphlet *An Ulster Reckoning*, but it is always heartbreaking to meet such sorrow on the ground; the dejection was palpable. During our previous tour, people had truly believed that the civil-rights agenda would redeem the North. But now, in the Boulevard Hotel in Newry, a group of young Catholic schoolteachers explained that they intended to leave the country as soon as they could, and probably head for Canada; we found the same growing hopelessness among young people throughout the North.

But we had a good time as well, attending the local markets, listening to fiery market-day preachers predicting hellfire, and drinking with a former flyweight boxer in a dismal hostelry in Lurgan. After our performance in Dungannon, once again before an audience of Gaels, an old girlfriend of mine from Glencull brought us back to her house for a party, and John was so much at ease that he danced, stiffly but resolutely, sporting a flashy weskit. But, as in Omagh, I was impressed – indeed depressed – by how little Hewitt seemed to know about the North of Ireland west of the River Bann, which a geographer had called 'the heartland of Ulster'.

But I could not have wished for a better travelling companion. Although notoriously crusty, John also showed flashes of wry humour, like sunlight on winter ice. He professed to be greatly amused by my need for an injection of Dutch courage before our rather formal readings. For me, a stammerer, those glancing calls at the pub before a performance were an essential ritual, and in a later poem by John (set in that pub in Lurgan), he speaks of 'the tall poet, his speech haunted by a stammer' – which shows that he understood my plight. At the time, though, he teased me, christening me 'the droughty Gael'. (It was the same droll compassion I had glimpsed in his treatment of E. M. Forster in Coventry.)

I showed him my hidden Ulster: touchstones like Knockmany Hill, which I had climbed as a boy, and near Dungannon, the coronation place of the O'Neills at Tullyhogue. I had the manuscript of *The Rough Field* with me, and he read it with pleasure and recognition, declaring at our final reading, at the Arts Council in the heart of Belfast, that 'it does for the North what MacDiarmid's *Drunk Man* did for Scotland'. This was a heartening and timely salute, after long years of toil. At my instigation, he himself had privately published the sequence of overtly political poems, *An Ulster Reckoning*, which had drawn some friendly fire. It was a brave enough act, since he, like myself, was contemplating returning to our riven island after years of deliberate exile:

Although it is my native place
and dear to me for many associations,
how can I return to that city
from my exile among strangers?

In a letter to me, he described the nature of his dilemma:
'My trouble is that I stand between the opposites, an interloper
to the Gaels with only four hundred years of Irish earth on my
bones, and a disaffected person to the Stormont bullies.' I would
like to think that our double tour helped assuage his fears, and
that he began to sense that slight but growing audience which
would sustain his later years back in Belfast, in Stockman's Lane.

Two final images haunt me from our Poets' Circuit. For me,
the supreme talisman of my home territory or native place is the
unmarked passage grave of Seskilgreen, locally called McRory's
Fort, after the family who have worked those fields forever.
('Clan Ruadhri or Rory' is an old name from the ancient Irish for
the Tagues of Tyrone, like my Cardinal relation whose portrait
Hewitt had drily dismissed on our first meeting.) I was extremely moved to show John this numinous place from my own tradition. It was late spring, and we ambled through the high grass,
past saucer-eyed cattle, then heaved ourselves over a series of
sturdy farm gates, and finally came upon it, little changed in its
five-thousand-year sleep. The big central stones, delicately
whorled, were warm with sunlight, and a bird had built its nest
in a crevice. We stood gazing together in a deep, shared silence,
and I remembered some lines of Hewitt, surmising and sum-
marising our heritage:

. . . what you seek may be no more than
a broken circle of stones on a rough hillside, somewhere.

The other powerful memory, for me, was the short period
we spent in Derry. It was, after all, where I had first come to
Ireland after the long voyage from Brooklyn. So I read the whole

of 'A New Siege', knowing full well that it would certainly annoy part of the audience, but unable to resist the provocation:

> twin races petrified
>   the volcanic ash
> of religious hatred

That morning, I had brought John to see Fountain Street, a working-class Protestant area of 'Londonderry' that was so Protestant, the kerbs were painted red, white and blue. He professed never to have seen the like, although later such blazoning of belief would show on murals and fluttering banners all over Ulster: the Irish tricolour and the Union Jack, and even the Palestinian and Israeli flags!

Amongst the audience in what I would still call 'Derry' was the playwright Brian Friel, who registered every reaction around him with seismic accuracy. 'They didn't like that Derry bit,' he said afterwards as we were having a drink together, shaking what I privately called 'the Great Friel Head'. He had clearly enjoyed himself, and was now relaxing over an amber whiskey. Brian in conversation begins slowly, almost haltingly, but when he warms up it is hard to stop him. But then I am in awe of playwrights, who, though often soft-spoken themselves, can make others speak in divers tongues.

Brian seems to me the most ambitious Irish playwright since Eugene O'Neill, always prepared to challenge an audience. Before we left, he ventured a note of caution or criticism. 'Why did you have to tour wearing labels like that, the Planter and the Gael?' he demanded with a snort. 'Why didn't you just go round as yourselves, John Hewitt and John Montague? Not wearing placards like sandwich-men!' It was an intriguing and sobering comment, especially coming from the future director of the Field Day Theatre Company.

Part IV

6

'Shine, Perishing Republic'

An Elegy for 1960s America

All through the 1960s, I kept up with my widening circle of friends in America. I had decided against returning to teach in Berkeley, which was in danger of becoming my Lotus Land, but this did not mean I could – or wished to – sunder all my connections to the strange, vast country where I had been born. Besides, UCD had also disappointed me, with the move to desolate Belfield imminent, and damp Dublin a comedown after warm California.

So I had returned to my base in Paris, and during the late sixties, when the time seemed right, ventured forth on reading tours throughout the United States. (And of course American friends and colleagues, from New York to Berkeley, wrote, rang and sometimes called at our little studio in the Fourteenth Arrondissement. I recall Tom Parkinson, looking alarmingly tall amongst the slight and slender Gauls, gulping brandy at our round table. Two other Toms, Flanagan and Redshaw, also descended. The former was already a successful novelist, while Redshaw was an endearing and bespectacled student, engaged in an ever-exfoliating thesis on myself, which made me feel at once elated and guilty.)

Before leaving Berkeley, I had gone with Gary Snyder and Lew Welch to a marvellous party at Ken Kesey's house. He himself was away, probably rollicking through America in his famous Love Bus, but we had a great time nevertheless. There was an enormous bowl of innocent-looking punch, crackling with dry ice, and, of course, the sweet-acrid fumes of pot and hash seasoned the air. As for sex, the scene was like the bawdy 'Ballad of Killemuir', with action everywhere, overflowing from the bedrooms, down the stairs and into the garden. Next morning, we played nude hopscotch on the beach, which I recommend as a cure for the cloudy mind.

A little while later, when I was safely ensconced back in Paris, a friend wrote from San Francisco: 'I've just been to a Sunday afternoon party at the House of the Dead (the Grateful Dead, of course). The scene was set by a bearded weirdo pitching about buck-naked on a big motorcycle. Lots of girls wandered around, also naked, hippie chicks with their babies. We were all stoned out of our minds. John, you should have been here.' Roughly around the same time, Robert Bly wrote as well, saying he had been to Haight-Ashbury, where he had seen stoned young women with balloons tied to their toes. But I was determined not to return to that wild Berkeley scene. The Californians, so restive and mobile, without society in the European sense, had tempted me, but I had already decided that it would be unwise to stay:

> Moving from the cool to the hot pool
> I follow a star flashing across the sky;
> No, not a star, but an incoming plane,
> With, yes, there beyond it, the evening star!
> If I stayed here longer, I would no longer
> Know what abiding things are.

On the Road Again
or 'Po-Biz'

So the answer did seem to be that newly glamorous phenomenon, the reading tour, a fashion launched by Dylan Thomas, who would also be its first martyr. But before his descent, he had warmed up the prairies with his plangent Welsh voice, 'a gong booming over a sea of treacle', to quote himself.

Of course European writers had read in America before. Charles Dickens, proud of his acting abilities, had barnstormed through the States, as had Oscar Wilde, enthralling the miners of Virginia City. And Yeats had helped to subsidise the Abbey Theatre and his prodigal father (two very different burdens) by his highly organised reading and lecture tours in America.

But it was the 'poetry circuit', or poetry as business ('po-biz', as it was now called), which was new. Suddenly poetry readings had become attractive and lucrative for both the academy and any number of visiting poets. A poet could travel from sea to shining sea, hopping from campus to campus, always sure of a warm welcome and copious refreshment. This flattered the vanity of the poet-performer, sold a few books, and leavened the atmosphere of some isolated academic community. I had devised my own eccentric gear for these occasions: I brandished a large silver ring which looked like a 'knuckleduster' and always provoked comment. (But the only person who divined the bird it depicted – a diving gannet – was Ted Hughes.) I also carried a hip flask of spirits: once, trying – and failing – to get a rise out of some particularly moribund rural audience, I produced the flask, declaring, 'Well, at least somebody is going to enjoy themselves', and took an enlivening sup.

With all the energy of unspent pious youth, I hurled myself across the Atlantic, a latter-day version of the wandering minstrel. I do not wish to paint too rosy a picture of such adventures, like Eric Linklater's *Juan in America*. Long-distance travel is exhausting: the transatlantic flight, often followed by a bus or train journey to some remote campus, meant that one did not always arrive as fresh as a daisy. And to be welcomed by people who know your name and are glad to greet you can be awkward, if you are trying to discern their name and rank through a film of fatigue. Also, in such a diverse country, you must quickly learn the subjects to avoid or focus on, depending on the location and affiliation of your particular host college. One could find oneself in a Jesuit college, a Southern Baptist university, an exclusive private college for young men or women, or a state school with an egalitarian spirit. That was the point of the bird ring and hip flask: to provoke lively exchanges with such varied audiences.

And sometimes you were just an excuse for a relaxation in academic routine. Once, I came to a small but prestigious New England college. Before the reading, I dutifully attended a cocktail party, ostensibly held in my honour, at the University Club. As the faculty meandered about, rattling the ice in their glasses, an elderly professor collared me. 'Do you know this fellow Montague?' he asked affably. 'I've never heard of him, but I guess he's as good an excuse as any for a party.' Then, 'Have a drink yourself', he suggested, gesturing to a black waiter in a master-to-flunkey manner. An hour later, we shambled into a pleasant though too-ample dinner, of roast beef with fairly good wines. There was no place card for 'Montague', but I slipped into an empty seat and found myself between 'Anglo-Saxon' and 'Middle English'. Another hour later, flushed and vaguely smiling, they all shuffled down to the lecture hall, filing into the front seats to settle their hands over their busily digesting stomachs and promptly fall asleep, while a nervous graduate student introduced me.

On another occasion, I travelled into the mountains of North Carolina with some friends, to a campus which had been snowbound for several months. I wondered why the audience were looking impatiently at their watches before I was halfway through, but finally understood that I was merely the alibi for a party, a thaw that seemed to take all night. I had developed a strategy for such endurance tests, hiding a bottle of bourbon behind a potted plant – not as Joyce had secreted his white wine in Foucquet's, for a snifter on the way to the toilet, but as an attempt to measure my own flagons, so that I would not succumb too heavily to the party spirit. My genial host, a fine painter in whose studio we were carousing, spotted my ruse, and substituted a nearly empty bottle of inferior bourbon for my fine George Dickel.

This particular party was so sprawling because everyone around me was suffering from cabin fever after months of snowy isolation, and they were more inclined to get bombed than to indulge in amorous play, or even to hobnob with the visiting writer. Finding myself on my own amidst the swirl of partying students and teachers, I wandered out of the smoky studio to inhale the frosty air, and watched a lean cat pick its way disdainfully from stone to stone along a cleared path. 'That's the only pussy you're going to see around here tonight', came the painter's chuckling voice over my shoulder.

Reluctant Rogue, Part Two

Indeed the opportunity for dalliance on such occasions has been overplayed. As well as the speaker often arriving late and tired, there is also the plane, train or bus to catch the next morning. And many American campuses, especially the rural private colleges, are more or less hermetically sealed: small, gossip-laden communities in which a student or staff member would feel reluctant to engage in some stray encounter that might echo unpleasantly. And yet the visiting bard was half-expected to misbehave in those days, à la Dylan Thomas. Eager poetry-reading students and august professors, cocooned in their academic fastnesses, actually wanted a glimpse of a legendary hard-drinking, wild Celtic troubadour, their textbooks come alive and kicking. All this would change, of course, as the freedoms of the sixties began to seem destructive, and the corporate world moved even into the academy.

Still, there were some sweet encounters along the way. I lurch gratefully to my lonely bed to sleep the sleep of the just, having performed fairly well and spoken civilly to students and staff. Towards dawn, I am awakened in my celibate bed in the faculty guest house, as a slender body slides in beside me. It is a young girl I had noticed at some point during the evening. She is by way of being a writer, a fledgling journalist on the student newspaper. 'I have come to comfort you,' she declares. 'You said that you were of Ulster Catholic background, and your Pope has just died!'

She did comfort me, but when I asked her to stay, she rebuffed me playfully. 'It's greedy to ask for too much comfort,' she said. Before she slipped away, I asked her name. She smiled serenely. 'I am Aurora, because I appeared with the dawn.' I would never see this whimsical creature again. This was part of the wistful charm of some of those strange encounters on the road. At best, they were utterly self-contained and even tender, neither cynical nor salacious.

Myth and reality met for me again during those days, at a famous Eastern women's college. There was a party afterwards in the house of the bearded young poet who had invited me. I fell into conversation with a very young, striking-looking girl who was balanced on a table, indolently swinging her legs. 'I love this house,' she volunteered airily. 'I had my first affair here.' Considering her extreme youth, I was slightly scandalised, and inquired, 'Affair? You're so young! With whom?'

'Oh, a middle-aged professor with grey hair like yours.'

Wryly amused, I asked her name. She promptly and suitably replied, 'Why, I'm Aphrodite. From the Greek, you know.'

What was I to make of these clever and lively American college girls? They were, on the one hand, casually disdainful of their parents' puritanical society, and utterly unlike the sedate university 'co-eds' of only a few years before. Sexually liberated, outspoken, and scornful of old-fashioned politesse, they personified what many consider the very spirit of the 1960s. Yet they also seemed to love the rich cargo of myth and legend that had been conveyed to them through their studies of the Classics and the European traditions, even if on occasion they distorted those myths for their own purposes. From Rose Twirlaleaf's demand that I should initiate her into the Mysteries, to those glancing manifestations of Aurora and the goddess Aphrodite, I was struck by the number of young women who seemed to balance their very American ideas of freedom and entitlement with a sense of the archetypal.

But the whole problem of the sixties and seventies, in

America and elsewhere, was the growing conflict between liberty and licence. While it was splendid that the hidebound fifties had been challenged by an increasingly politicised generation, that same generation was failing to learn the limits and responsibilities of freedom. A painter friend of mine, an 'amorous man', as Yeats describes Cuchulain, gave me a warning as I was setting off on an American tour. 'Remember, John,' he said, rephrasing Pascal, 'that while the heart may have its reasons, which reason does not know, the prick also has its reasons, that the heart does not know!' And he gave a grim, cautionary laugh.

One cannot underestimate the influence of a minute tablet – called, simply, the Pill – on the sexual mores of that time. Suddenly, women were released from fear and repression into relative erotic freedom. I say 'relative' because, in that pre-feminist age, women were by and large expected to be just 'chicks', biddable objects for men, who chastened them for being 'uptight' if they expressed reservations or reluctance when it came to sex, or a desire for tenderness. And no one seemed to realise then that it was potentially quite dangerous for women to be ingesting vast quantities of hormones as a form of contraception.

My generous friend New York socialite Bananas O'Rourke was an extreme example of how the freedoms won in the 1960s could curdle into something unpleasant, even nasty, especially perhaps where women were concerned. Poor-Little-Rich-Girl Bananas was a soft target, subsidising all kinds of wilder ventures, like the 'Fuck You Press'. She had been almost strangled by William Burroughs, had searched with Robert Lowell under the bed for his glasses, and had listened through the long nights to the manic soliloquies of William Gaddis Junior – all brilliant men. One day, though, she bashfully showed me a cheque she had just received, inscribed to 'the most-laid hostess of the year' from a magazine she had been supporting. I supposed that this tasteless joke was part of the sexual flippancy, the archness, which prevailed at the time, and which was meant to seem daring and renegade. It struck me as merely heartless, bereft of either bravery or wit.

I SEE CRIMSON

A major preoccupation for me in the late sixties was, of course, what was happening back home. News of the forces and changes that were 'breaking moulds' in my native Ulster had already begun to trickle into the academy. In 1970, I travelled down from a reading organised by the Swallow Press in Chicago to an American conference of Irish Studies meeting in Carbondale, Illinois, where my old pal, Tom Kinsella, had moved. The conference's main theme was the North, because of recent events; Seamus Heaney was there as well.

There was the usual tension between the many academics and the visiting writers (a poet or writer can feel like the pig in the bacon factory when surrounded by scholars). And a round-table discussion on Ulster turned deadly serious when Mary O'Malley, the brave founder of the Lyric Theatre in Belfast and editor of *Threshold*, attacked the Professor of History from Queen's University, J. C. Beckett. She complained about his obvious bias against the Republic and its ethos, as the nettled historian tried to declare his impartiality – which I am afraid I was also inclined to doubt.

Seamus Heaney was his usual diplomatic self, trying to smooth ruffled feathers, but when it came to my turn I was asked what future I saw for the North. Thinking of Kinsella's heroic translation of the Táin, I recalled a passage where the attacking army meets the woman poet and prophet Fedelimh, a Celtic Cassandra. Asked what the future holds for Ulster, she intones her sorrowful, blood-drenched vision: 'I see crimson./ I see red.' Bleak lines I had tried to translate myself.

I found myself similarly possessed, repeating her prophesy almost verbatim, though adding a Joycean 'hosts of the dead' and declaring, nearly despite myself, that I saw no future for the North but the shedding of blood. My words shocked even myself, while the hall began to buzz, released from its polite academic torpor. I had expressed a vision of violence untempered by the usual palliatives and earnestly expressed hopes for peace, and it no doubt seemed, in that setting, excessive and unseemly. Challenged by the audience to explain myself, I could not but repeat that the only future I saw for my province was a river of blood.

'How can you possibly say something as awful as that?' one academic cried, and for the rest of the conference people avoided me as if I were a leper clanging his harsh warning bell. But, alas, I was to be proven right.

I found a home from home in Pierre Trudeau's Canada, more specifically in Toronto, where I became bosom friends with a young poet and writer, Barry Callaghan, son of Morley Callaghan, the august Canadian novelist. Morley had the same London publisher as myself, Tim O'Keeffe at MacGibbon & Kee, and I liked his taut, austere style: he had been a friend of the young Hemingway not only in Toronto but also in Paris, where he had even 'decked' him in a famous friendly boxing bout at the American Center.

Morley's son Barry was a flamboyant character, a man possessed of almost too many talents. Not only was he a fluent writer in both prose and verse, he was also a journalist in print and television. And he had founded a magazine called *Exile*, which would grow into a small publishing company, Exile Editions. He conducted his life like a Renaissance prince: he owned a farmhouse in south-western Ontario which included a romantically mouldering chapel, and an entire small island in Georgian Bay, in Ontario, as well as a billet in his father's house in Toronto's fashionable Rosedale. To lie in the lukewarm waters of Lake Huron, off Snake Island, and listen to the crying of the loon, was strangely moving, as was glimpsing a bear shamble away from the local garbage dump like a large brown giant, licking its paws.

What I loved about Toronto was how it seemed like a Belfast that had swerved in the right direction. It was northern, chilly and full of Protestants, but it was growing as ebullient and wild as New Orleans. In Canada, somewhere along the line, the

Protestant ethic had been leavened by the hippie *Zeitgeist*. There were pedestrian streets where the pleasure-seekers surged; jazz clubs and ethnic restaurants, a lively spirit along the waterfront (which would become the venue for one of the world's best poetry-reading series, 'Harbourfront'), and loads of young men and women determined to enjoy themselves.

I gave a reading in a hippie commune in Yorkville. The commune was a large apartment house divided into whimsical Olympian sections – 'The Aphrodite Suite', 'The Zeus Chambers', 'The Apollo Hall' – another example of myth adorning reality. My audience were stoned, of course, and I was a little 'over the top' myself. But they seemed genial, without that hint of menace which I had begun to feel in the hippie enclaves of San Francisco and New York. Clearly they were a bit behind the times, but were all the better for that. They spirited me back to Haight-Ashbury or the East Village before the hippie movement had soured and the hard drugs had moved in. I could not help wondering if the old hippie potion of pot, hash and free love – that variation on the pipe of peace – would not do a world of good for drear Belfast, and indeed our whole frozen North. In a way, Canada, with cosmopolitan cities like Toronto, Montreal and Vancouver, seemed to offer me the first real temptation to an easier alternative life since my idyllic Berkeley days. It was the New World, but sweetened by a lingering European atmosphere of refinement and gentility. The people struck me as saner than the Americans, better-mannered and softer-voiced.

I also thought that women had a better deal in Canada than across the border. I taught a summer school in Toronto which was composed of secondary-school teachers, mainly women. I had found, in the States, that schoolteachers were not held in high esteem, except at university level, where they were mostly men. But in Canada, teachers at the secondary and even primary levels were well respected, with a definite place in the community and a decent salary. And there were special incentives for those who wished to replenish their teaching skills and store of knowledge by taking summer courses, like mine on contemporary poetry. Or they could travel further north to teach and work with the Inuits.

Altogether, Canadian women seemed much more independent and confident than their American sisters, and the men impressed me generally as more gentle, less driven and less macho than their neighbours to the south. Crossing the border into upstate New York, you heard a different language, peppered with profanities like 'goddamn' and the ever-present 'asshole'. Puzzled by this linguistic border crossing, I speculated that 'asshole' was similar to the Irish 'eejit' or that other Americanism, 'jerk', though harsher and more contemptuous. And I could not understand why such a useful part of the anatomy should be so maligned – except that there must have been, in the States, a deep homophobia, something I also did not find as much in Canada.

Profanity, when spoken or written in the right place, can be powerful, startling and irreverent. And it can also serve as a relatively harmless safety valve for anger, as in the stylised exchange of insults I had got used to along the French roads. But I have already observed that, while a French driver may try to blacken the name of your sister, or throw scathing invectives at your own poor head, he would seldom invoke your mother, whereas in America the term 'motherfucker' seemed far more ubiquitous than either 'please' or 'thank you'. The rather brutal style of American profanity also struck me as being the product of an anti-intellectual society, where a good command of language would be considered effete in certain circles; as if 'goddamn' or 'asshole' were the only descriptive words one could – or should – muster.

There were other saving graces in Canada. The Chinatown of Toronto, and the more splendid one in the Pacific city of Vancouver, could officially have direct trade with mainland China, which meant a plethora of culinary marvels, including one-thousand-year-old preserved eggs, aromatic spices and exotic mushrooms. Toronto was a lakeshore city like Chicago, land-bound but with a mysterious connection to the winds and humours of the Great Lakes, yet it was much less abrasive. Across the Toronto skyline, lights gleamed like computer panels, and I thought of all those plucky, independent women I had taught, living within those lighted spaces, in their own apartments, something still more or less unheard of back in Ireland, and even to some degree in the States. Also, there did not seem to be the same racial tensions, or street violence. As I was leaving my publishers, Swallow, in Chicago, my editor asked where I was going. I replied that I was strolling down to join Nelson Algren at a bar in the Sheraton. 'Don't walk,' he admonished, although it was only a few blocks. 'You might not get there. There's a lot of heroin downtown.' Yet I loved rambling with Barry Callaghan through night-time Toronto, feeling in no obvious peril.

SHINE, PERISHING REPUBLIC

Swallow Press had moved to Chicago from Denver, and wished to take on two of my books, *A Chosen Light* and *Tides*, so I went there to see my old friend Nelson Algren and do a radio interview for the famous Studs Terkel.

This was not my first visit to Chicago. I had been brought there by my friends Judge Macallister (father of that red-headed poet Claire, who had descended on Dublin) and his wife Dorothy in 1956, for the Democratic National Convention. It was an extraordinary event, half raucous circus (Estes Kefauver sporting his coonskin cap), half American Hall of Fame. I stood in a line to shake hands with the likes of Averell Harriman, Eleanor Roosevelt and, of course, the candidate himself, the battle-weary intellectual Adlai Stevenson. For a few minutes at the end of the conference, the spotlights suddenly shone on one of the handsomest young couples I had ever seen, a smiling, relaxed young Irish-American called John F. Kennedy and his lovely dark-haired wife, Jackie, both as glamorous as movie stars. Clearly these assembled Democrats considered them their shining future.

But within the next ten years, the thoughtful Stevenson would be defeated by the great Ike, the handsome man I had glimpsed would be struck down in Dallas, the South would erupt with civil-rights protests, and countless American soldiers would kill or be slaughtered in the jungles of south-east Asia.

On that night in 1956, the country had seemed eager, indefatigable, still charged with a lingering post-war optimism. Yet now I was riding to a big protest reading in Milwaukee on behalf of the Chicago Seven, which included that sixties icon Abbie Hoffman. One of my pals from Iowa, the poet Robert Bly, was chairman for the evening, and friends from San Francisco, like Robert Duncan, were also there, to chant their charms against that evil war in Vietnam and the civil injustices at home. It was an electric occasion, though very different from the hopeful Democratic Convention of 1956.

Now, I was surrounded by exhausted, embittered, angry people who felt that their country had betrayed not only them but the world. It was as if this great country had been stricken by a self-inflicted plague, leaving only the universities, like feudal walled cities or medieval monasteries, as sanctuaries against the encircling darkness, and the poets, like monks, chanting their spells. A hellish combination of an insane war that could not be won and the unresolved race issue had produced this poisonous brew. Madeleine and I had seen the black singer Odetta break down during a concert in Paris, admitting tearfully that she could not sing any more because she was so worried about her people.

And considering the series of assassinations of the best and brightest, it was hard not to believe in a right-wing conspiracy driven by fundamentalists. While the Ku Klux Klan, exulting in their absurd bedsheets, and burning crosses, were no longer so evident, their mentality was still ubiquitous. Poisoned lands, indeed! I had come back to an America of poisoned cities.

Robert Bly called on me to speak from the floor. And again, as in Carbondale, I found myself intoning in an almost incantatory way, as if anger and anguish were channelling through me, like the American poets of my own generation whom I had just heard. I quoted from the section of my expanding *Rough Field* called 'The Bread God', which tries to confront the low-church Protestant loathing of the Catholic Mass, with its consecrated wafer and chalice. It was as if, almost unconsciously, I had struck a chord, as people began to comment excitedly. Both Bly and

Duncan agreed that the real problem with America was its need to face down its messianic Protestantism. 'It lies behind all this slaughter,' cried one of the Roberts. 'We do believe that this is God's Own Country, which gives us licence to be xenophobic and to do anything to anybody. They're all gooks to us!'

The other Robert chorused in. 'We cry "God Bless America", but then we destroy it, desecrating the landscape with highways and lookalike shopping centres from sea to shining sea. Our increasingly bleak, empty cities and countryside are a reflection of a sickness in our spirit, the Protestant ethic gone mad, as we ravage the country for commerce. Robinson Jeffers was right in his condemnation, "While this America settles in the mould of its vulgarity, heavily thickening to empire . . .".'

I remembered how, ten or so years before, when we were both students at Iowa, Robert Bly had presented a workshop with poems displaying a wild, strange, angry vision of a despoiled America. Sometimes he had sounded like a hellfire preacher. And Robert Duncan had invoked the prophetic vision of Whitman, contrasting it, like Allen Ginsberg in *The Fall of America*, with the urban desolation of much of contemporary America. A famous European scholar, Mario Praz, on his way to give a lecture in Detroit, had wakened from a snooze on the train and, staring out at the decaying houses and tattered billboards, had cried out: 'What's all this nonsense about the atom bomb? It has already fallen!'

Again I spent a week in San Antonio, conducting a seminar and listening to the list of murders on the radio every morning – usually of another Mexican who had been dumped in the river. With a bunch of the male students, I crossed into Mexico, to one of those ramshackle border towns which was run like a big brothel. The cowpokes went to an enormous dance hall called 'Boystown', where you could dance with a local girl before retiring with her to the maze of shacks behind: ten bucks a throw! Many of the girls wore religious medals or crucifixes round their necks, as they had in Barcelona's Barrio Chino. In a better part of town, the ranchers paraded with comely, perhaps convent-educated, girls, whose company, I was told, could be bought for the weekend for one hundred dollars. All this did not look so different from the brothel quarters of Barcelona or Lisbon, except that I was uncomfortably aware of the racist aspect, as if Mexicans could be bought or sold like cattle. I thought again of Bly's words about the Protestant ethic gone wrong.

We drove back to a small Texan village on the edge of a big ranch. It was Saturday night, and the cowboys – shit-kickers, as they were affectionately known – were whooping it up on raw bar bourbon. (I felt as if I were in a dismal pub in some desolate North of Ireland town, like the infamous Mac's of Fintona, where the name was written backwards in some hopeless attempt at wit, but which accurately reflected the state of mind of most of its clients.) There were very few women; the air seemed thick with male restlessness, and I gathered that the evening usually ended in a brawl. I spoke to the local police chief, a large man, calm as the eye of a hurricane.

'Oh,' he said affably, 'the boys get a bit excited come Saturday night, and try to kill each other.'

'So how do you stop them?' I asked, impressed by this big man's equanimity.

He indicated a canister riding on his belt, a can I recognised from civil-rights marches in the North of Ireland. 'First,' he answered, 'I just spray both of 'em with this here mace, before they hurt each other too bad. But that can be dangerous, because then they might both turn on me. And two riled cowboys is quite a handful.' He paused, smiling.

'So what do you do then?' I asked, persisting.

He patted the Colt in its holster. 'I might have to pretend to draw this. And if I do, I bring them away for a night's rest in our little iron hotel next to the courthouse.'

'But what if they don't listen, even when you've drawn the gun? Or what if they run away?'

With a sigh, he gestured me outside, unlocking the boot of his car, to produce a gleaming rifle. 'They know that's there. So they don't run too far. I'm known to be the best shot in town.'

I avoided Berkeley like a guilty lover abandoning his sweetheart, even going instead to read at the University of California in Los Angeles. But I did allow myself to return once, and permitted myself a nostalgic walk down Telegraph Avenue, where, out of the blue, I heard an all-too-familiar wheedling voice. It was a married Rose Twirlaleaf, with a baby on her hip! I asked where her husband was, and she answered, with her customary airiness, 'He's away somewhere, but he'll come back.'

'What's he like?' I asked, trying to imagine her consort, the father of the chubby infant I was now inspecting. But all she said by way of character reference was, 'Oh, he's the kind of guy that takes no shit.'

Rose offered to drive me around for the day, and I visited yet another poetical Robert, Creeley this time, in a commune north of Berkeley. He too was stoned out of his mind, and said sagely, 'John, my new bag is *people*.' Then, to vary the diet, I called at the high-security prison nearby, San Quentin. A French friend was on a programme for helping prisoners with long-term, even death, sentences, and I knew the name of the inmate with whom she had been corresponding there. Growing up in the North, I was not unused to visiting prisons, but the nervous intensity of an American high-security jail was different. The very air clanged with dread.

The prisoner told me he had not killed anybody; it had just been an accident. But then he said it was hard to keep one's temper in the jail, where guards and prisoners were equally tough and macho. I signed a copy for him of 'A New Siege', the section of *The Rough Field* that I had read outside Armagh Jail when Bernadette Devlin was a prisoner there. I wondered what he and his fellow inmates would make of this meditation on historical violence. The one moment of levity was when I quoted a remark of my County Tyrone sage, Barney Horisk. 'You know, John,' he'd said solemnly, 'the advantage of calling on friends in prison is that they're always in.' Even my tense, surly American convict gave a guffaw at that shaft of rural wisdom.

*

Tom Parkinson, the Yeats scholar, kept pressing and pestering me to return to Berkeley, but I preferred this new pattern of brief, concentrated, flying visits. So I kept recommending my younger Northern contemporary, Seamus Heaney, especially since Seamus and his wife Marie were beginning to feel uneasy living in an increasingly tense Belfast with their two little boys. The novelist Tom Flanagan pitched in as well, even though he hated Parkinson, whom he regarded as a fashionable campus radical, whereas he, a stern conservative, thought that separation between students and staff should be strictly observed.

So Seamus and his family had the pleasant relief of the academic year 1970/71 in Berkeley. He wrote to me in high good humour about the contrast between balmy Berkeley and bleak Belfast – sentiments echoed in a piece he wrote for the *Listener*. Feeling very much the older brother, I wrote back to warn him that the gleaming surface of life in the Bay Area, the smell of eucalyptus and the ever-present sun, could conceal hidden dangers; as if shoals of rock and fierce currents lay beneath the shining expanse of water that reached out from Berkeley towards the Golden Gate.

And sure enough, Marie Heaney was nearly abducted in broad daylight – on New Year's Day, in fact – close to the university. Being a strong young Tyrone woman, she fought off her assailant, but of course it could have been serious. This mugging seemed to me part of the violence which now coursed beneath American life at every level, less obvious than in Belfast and the North, though more insidious because more random.

Around that time, I received more bad news from Berkeley. An old drinking buddy, a tall bearded poet called Lew Welch, had disappeared. He had wandered off from Gary Snyder's hand-built mountain home in the Low Sierras, above Nevada City, carrying a pistol. He had become depressed by a calamitous oil spill in the Bay, and by how little was being done about such an ecological disaster, especially as Northern California seemed, as it had for Robinson Jeffers, like a last stand, safe from rapacious capitalism. Had Lew not written: 'This is the last place, there/ is nowhere else to go'? And now he had wandered off himself, from 'the feet of the final cliffs'.

My pal had loped away like some forlorn cowboy in an old-fashioned Western, riding into the sunset.

> Lew, lost comrade,
> lover of the large, the small,
> climber of mountains,
> collator of graffiti,
> I relished laughing
> & talking with you,
> liquor warming the throat.
>
> But you wandered off
> in your buckskin outfit –
> a poetic Davy Crockett –
> a bardic Daniel Boone –
> to a crevasse where
> your friendly call
> was lost.

7

THE PEAR IS RIPE

OR SHALL WE OVERCOME?

> running voices
> streets of Berlin
> Paris, Chicago
> seismic waves
> zigzagging through
> a faulty world . . .

During the Algerian war, a press of students surged down the narrow canyon of the Rue Daguerre, chanting 'Le fascisme ne passera pas!' In the latter half of the sixties, student protests were spreading across the world: was this enthusiasm or infection? Although Algeria had achieved independence, the tensions fomented by that long and bitter struggle (which lasted from 1954 until 1962) still poisoned the French body politic; a heavily armed branch of the police force, the infamous CRS, was one of the legacies of the war.

I flew back from Dublin to Paris in May 1968, via Brighton, where I had heard Robert Duncan read, a dazzling marathon performance which lasted three hours: one hour reciting, one hour chanting, one hour singing, like the bubbling cauldron of a sorcerer. There had been no planning, only word of mouth, but disciples kept arriving from across England to hear their

174

poetical prophet. His rich style seemed to go with the lavish elegance of the Regency Pavilion, and the mouldering, camp glamour of the Promenade. And of course he sang of War.

Then, abruptly, I arrived back in a France that seemed on the verge of revolution. I had already been to several civil-rights marches in the San Francisco Bay Area, and the North of Ireland was just beginning to simmer. But even these marches had not prepared me for the drama, the intense street theatre, of Paris. There is a difference between marching and singing along a country road in Tyrone (or even facing a blue phalanx of police in Oakland), and the closing down of an entire great urban centre. And since I knew the geography of the Sorbonne, had indeed given a lecture on Goldsmith in one of its halls, I was able to wander along the margins of the action. Of course, May '68 is now as mythical as Easter 1916: if all who maintain they were there really had been, the rebels probably *would* have 'over-come'.

At first I was exhilarated by the energy, the spontaneous passion and the display of unity among the protesters. But gradually what began to strike me was that, while the idea of a revolution is intellectually glorious, the reality can mean a growing squalor. Rubbish collections had ceased, or at best become intermittent, so that the streets began to smell of rotting food. And in the area around the now-turbulent Sorbonne, many shops had closed, anxious owners hurriedly barricading their windows against the violence. So food was in short supply and, in a country of gourmets, where a disdain for tinned goods would usually prevail, there was, instead, a sudden rush on anything that was tinned or preserved. Inevitably, rats began to appear, and the bigger birds to swoop down like vultures on the bulging, burgeoning detritus. Knowing as I did the French attitude towards life's creature comforts, the student revolution began to seem doomed to me: deprive the modern middle-class Frenchman of good meals and wine – even if he is a leftist – and he would be bound to temper his high ideals. But May '68 had a profound effect on the private life as well, creating distance in the relationship between parents and children, and forging unexpected alliances between students of different classes, colours and backgrounds, and even, for a glorious while, the workers and the students. As Wordsworth cried: 'Bliss was it in that dawn to be alive,/ But to be young was very heaven!'

So how could I, as a poet, be immune to this tidal wave of emotion? It was as if the France I had slowly come to understand, the stable world of its provincial nobility, and Madeleine's upper-middle-class milieu at the Patronnat, had now been shorn of its imposing façade, revealing the frail scaffolding beneath. At one point, brandishing axe handles and clubs, the students stormed the gates of the Bourse, chanting: 'Temple of gold, Temple of gold!' Even President Charles de Gaulle, confronted with the anger of his own young, seemed to fumble, and actually disappeared for a few days to consult the army, as if the student revolt were part of some international plot.

Make Love Not War

As for myself, this ferocious desire for change was incarnated by the presence of someone, an Other. A young woman from Nanterre, the shabby new university on the outskirts of Paris where the revolt had begun, came to interview me for her student magazine. She was also looking for Peter Lennon, whose work she had read in the *Guardian*, especially a piece of his analysing the various kinds of French police, from the humble gendarme to the daunting CRS, or riot squad. I suppose that Peter and I were both Beckett substitutes but, in any case, I was in, while he was away.

Evelyn, a student leader, was full of stories about the riots around the Sorbonne, and of police violence: we might well have been in the same amphitheatre at the same time, listening to the charismatic Dany the Red or the exhortations of Sartre. We shared our heady impressions, she from the inside, me from the outside, participant and observer, fired by the excitement of a period when, to quote Marx on the Eighth Brumaire, 'Men and things seemed set in sparkling diamonds, and each day's spirit is ecstatic.'

It affected me all the more directly because the Patronnat, where Madeleine worked, had become a target for protest and temporary occupation by some of the shock troops of the revolution. And now I was confronted by a representative of this new class war; she was also beautiful, and beauty, along with fiery youth, can be a powerful potion. I do not think we completed the interview: our conversation became too personal, though I think she did finally publish a version in an Irish newspaper.

But that afternoon we eyed each other with some incredulity. What do you do when destiny appears on your doorstep? Or was it destiny? Perhaps the turmoil I felt was just my longing for a new life superimposed on an 'Other', indeed a radiant and zealous Other, a perfect vessel to contain my own dreams. That is the danger of the 'muse theory': the poet as lover believes that he is responding to a power, but what he is glimpsing may be merely a projection of his own dream – of liberation, of renewal, of a second youth. And the other's actual self is obscured through the force of such dreams, dragged along by the chariot wheels of someone else's destiny. Or else the two people's dreams can mesh in a vision that is at once intoxicating and dangerous.

One powerful impression haunts me. As she shifted uneasily, tapping her pencil against her reporter's pad, I seemed to see a schism in her spirit, a division in her psyche, something polarised, like in a Picasso portrait. So two contradictory impulses wrestled in me: on the one hand, the desire to cherish and help the Lady; on the other, a strange feeling that whatever was happening, it was beyond me. (And there was something I realised only later: this girl, with her immense sad eyes and pearly skin, resembled my wistful-looking mother in her youth, a likeness that disturbed me, albeit unconsciously.) But above all, a mainly mocking voice chided me: 'So you're afraid to get involved with this young woman! It's too much for you, is it? I thought you believed that you poets could handle anything; instead, you reach for the white flag.'

A love affair began, and for as long as I could, I fought to control the overwhelming emotions it evoked. I imagine that she was as uncertain as myself about the implications of our relationship, yet we seemed unable to greet and part in the best classic French style. On the other hand, French society itself had been briefly overturned, like the cobblestones in the streets and the burning cars, and what it revealed was a deep ennui, a crevasse between two ways of thinking, the old and the young, the right and the left. Indeed, the split I thought I had glimpsed in my young interviewer might really have been a vision of a polarised representative of a polarised society. French society is so volatile, so tensely divided, that the French develop formal structures to control the emotions, which then erupt through those structures, like the roots of powerful trees buckling a footpath.

ON THE BARRICADES

With her brisk and brave rationality, Madeleine embodied one aspect of the Gallic character, one version of Marianne, but then there was passionate Marianne, storming the barricades, à la Delacroix, which an angry Evelyn, pelting the police with rocks, had come to symbolise for me. The explosive years of 1789 and 1848 stormed quickly from success to success, or lurched from disaster to disaster. Both these things happened during the French Revolution, from the killing of a king to the founding of a short-lived empire by a small, irascible genius from Corsica. But now there were also the media. May '68 was not only street theatre, but also instant cinema and television: the line of students facing the riot police was like something out of Eisenstein. And one's sympathy swung naturally to the fervent young facing the tear gas and the batons beneath the great sombre dome of the Pantheon, where the heroes of the Enlightenment slumbered.

Boulevard St Michel

The black flags
of the anarchists
between shafts of chill rain

summon demon powers
to defend the barricades
of cobblestones, sawn trunks
of chestnut trees
charred bodies of
family cars, dustbins.

Against everything,
for nothing but this destruction:
its cleansing, its terrible joy.
The Pantheon glows,
Les Invalides glowers,
Guevera's beard strangles Voltaire,

while the gadget-gorged
Citizen discovers in the looting flames
a lost religious awe!

But the mood, with its Blakean energy, was short-lived, like a rocket rising and falling, casting a strange sputtering light over the familiar city. Then there was the inevitable long period of assimilation, as society tried to estimate the achievements of such a period of storm and stress. May '68 never became as bloody as May 1881; although there were rumours of more student deaths than officially reported, they were never confirmed. Nor did it match the violence of the street fights during the Algerian War, and certainly not the Commune, when thirty thousand people died, and one-third of the city was burned. Neither was it a match for the confusions of 1848, charted by Flaubert in his most personal novel, *L'Education Sentimentale*, where his password for change is: 'The pear is ripe'.

Then there were attempts to reform the moribund French university system, like the experimental University of Vincennes. Some brilliant people were drafted there, such as Anthony Sampson, the British political commentator, and Christine Brooke-Rose, a young English writer experimenting with the *nouveau roman*. I taught there for a while – Contemporary American Poetry, and Irish Literature – and was subjected to periodic investigations by leftist student representatives, making sure that my curriculum had the correct political content. They distributed copies of Mao's Little Red Book, which, alas, reminded me of the Catechism of my Ulster Catholic youth. I remember their patient incomprehension as I played Joyce's voice reading a passage from *Finnegans Wake*. But then the May revolution had attracted many observers, all looking for something. I saw my French poet friend Michel Deguy scanning the walls of the Sorbonne for quotes for the next issue of his magazine, *Poésie*. And lo and behold, there again was the English poet whom I had last seen during the riots on the Berkeley campus. This time the penny dropped, and I did not ask him what he was doing there.

Most of us were poorly equipped to understand the to and fro that characterised the unexpected events of May '68; to some extent, we were all in our different ways 'riding the tiger'. At first, de Gaulle was bewildered, and he seemed to contemplate resignation, as a palpable rage surged through the streets of Paris. What was happening? What had he done wrong? Why were the young of his country (which he had navigated through defeat and Occupation into a new prosperity) so angry? Rumours of his possible abdication swept the country, leaving an opening for the wily François Mitterrand to offer himself to the nation, while others called for the return of Pierre Mendès-France, de Gaulle's predecessor as president. Or would the army, which had not been seen on the streets since the Algerian crisis, be summoned in to remedy matters with 'a whiff of grapeshot'?

The last option was unlikely, since the French Left was at the height of its power, representing nearly half the nation, with influential newspapers like *Humanité*, and intellectually eminent writers like Louis Aragon and Sartre. And when the workers of Renault and Citroën closed their gates, and appeared to be making common cause with the students, the very structure of French society seemed in peril. The climax was a parade of this assembled Left of students and workers down the Champs Élysées, that traditional French defile which had echoed with the tramp of German soldiers and the triumphant songs of the

Liberation. But it had never seen this kind of manifestation, half a million strong, chanting slogans and waving flags. Was the Conservative press correct in suggesting a *complot*, or plot, with the unions secretly subsidised by the Soviet Union? Or was it a red herring? The quashing of the Prague Revolution would show that the Soviets were now as reactionary and intolerant as their enemies on the Far Right. Anyway, the dream of an alliance between the Left and the young was beginning to fade.

Nevertheless, 'C R S – S S!' cried the furious students facing the police. They were undaunted by batons, helmets and even tear gas, and covered their faces with handkerchiefs soaked in water. They had become practised street fighters, hurling flag-stones at their enemy, who were so sheathed in leather and metal that they resembled giant insects. As Flaubert describes in *L'Education Sentimentale*, about the riots in 1848: 'The trees along the avenues, the public toilets, the benches, the grilles, the gas lamps, all were uprooted, toppled; Paris that morning was covered in barricades.'

De Gaulle dithered. And ironically, just as Daniel Cohn-Bendit was forbidden to cross into France as an 'alien', de Gaulle lofted himself away in a private helicopter to consult his faithful General Massu across the border in the lovely spa town of Baden-Baden, in Dany the Red's other country, Germany. Massu has since said that they also discussed Corneille; in any case, de Gaulle certainly came back reassured that there was no military plot unfurling all the way from the Kremlin into the hallowed halls of the Sorbonne. Indeed the Soviets were dismayed by the potential for disruption that these student movements represented. Soon they would invoke the Warsaw Pact to quash the Velvet Revolution.

The alliance between the students and the workers could not really last, because of their different aims. The workers were mainly concerned with the 'SMIG', or the cost-of-living index,

while the students had the luxury of their high ideals being subsidised. And of course the Right swiftly learnt from the Left, so
that, soon, the Champs Élysées was once more swollen with a
mass demonstration. This time it was of a different hue altogether, far less colourful and droll, the middle class in coats and
ties, with André Malraux, a veteran of the Spanish Civil War and
the Resistance, leading, waving a tiny flag. Some time later, I saw
a marvellously avuncular analysis by the great giraffe himself, de
Gaulle, claiming, with a kindly shrug, that he understood all too
well the humours of the young. After all, he had been to blame,
because he had provided them with a flourishing society that
indulged their callow dreams of revolt.

Many of my elders who had been through more extreme and
dangerous situations felt the same. Beckett, who had been
involved in the Resistance, seemed to dismiss the protests with
a wry shrug, although he was vaguely sympathetic to the actor
and director Jean-Louis Barrault's dramatic opening of the
Odeon to the students. Our own Irish dragon, that old gunman
turned commissar, Todd Andrews, wrote anxiously to Madeleine
from Dublin: 'I was worried about you – not about the physical
danger, because I felt and thought at the time that the chances
of a revolution where guns came out was negligible; I thought a
lot of the rioting in Paris was posturing, in the manner of the
greylag geese . . . . I have thought a lot about the student unrest.
I think much of it is imitative and infectious. I think, as far as I
know anything about the Sorbonne, that conditions there are
foul beyond measure and probably the students had every right
to kick about their treatment, but when they extend their activities and pretend to leadership in the manner of Dany the Red, I
part company with them, as indeed did the Communists.'

And old Todd reserved a kindly rebuke for myself. 'John, of
course, in a muddle-headed way, is all in favour of the students,
and he gave a very good interview on television, where he hoped

the students would start unrest here. What have they to start unrest about? What beats me about the whole situation is the general assumption that students and youth have by some big afflatus received wisdom superior to their elders.'

Such patronising dismissals of the young rebels, as if they were all merely pampered, tantrum-throwing brats, astonished me then and continues to do so now. In addition, it seems that, since the 1960s, every reactionary government throughout Europe and the States have realised how dangerous it is to educate their young people. Education emboldens them to think independently and to challenge authority – which should be the purpose of learning and the foundation of any democracy. Yet funding for schools, and standards of education, have fallen so sharply in recent years that illiteracy has become a major problem in countries that are awash with wealth, like the United States. It is as though there is a tacit agreement among conservative powers that the young should be kept ignorant, in order to prevent the revolts that altered the landscape of the sixties, from Berkeley to Paris, from ever happening again. And ironically, the young Todd Andrews had been a rebel himself, not only against England, but against the pro-Treaty government in Ireland: a stormy petrel indeed.

I cannot entirely disagree, however, with his criticisms of the 'revolting students'. Largely the children of privilege, like their kindred spirits in Berkeley and Columbia, they were heady with leftist ideals. But their exuberance, and the festive spirit they created with their defiant parades, could not conceal the fact that at least some of them were *playing* at revolution, without understanding the wider implications, both political and social, of their actions. But something that stands out is how Europe absorbed and assimilated its young revolutionaries, while America thrust theirs out into the margins. Somehow Europe was able to encompass the ideology of its angry students, and make it part of the mainstream political scene. The States, by contrast, have remained more inflexible and right-wing, their social policies largely untempered by influences from the Left.

EXIT KAFKA

In the midst of all this turbulence, our beloved cat, Kafka, sickened and died. An elegant, slender Siamese, he had lived the life of a Gallic Reilly for nearly a decade. He had no ladies to court, being cut, and no mice to catch, since our studio was pest-free, so his activity was restricted to a scamper in the courtyard or a race up and down the studio stairs. He listened respectfully as I chanted my verses (if he was not asleep), and purred if touched. Sometimes he lifted his head to attend my phone calls, or if the concierge came knocking at our door, but mostly he slumbered.

At night, he slept at the bottom of the marriage bed. If we became 'matrimonially involved', he managed to ride the storm, sometimes balancing on my back. And of course he travelled with us to the countryside, peering intently through the car window as we hurtled along through French traffic. Altogether, he was as deeply involved in our lives as an animal could be. Madeleine's mother was a bit shocked by our devotion to our feline, who was so obviously a surrogate for the children we could not have, yet Kafka really was a cat of remarkable sensibility.

But now he was ill, and so began my afternoon pilgrimages to our neighbourhood vet. I had a fine large briefcase, which I used for UCD lectures or American tours, and into this capacious bag I inserted an anxious cat instead. Sometimes I managed to march the whole way, and Kafka seemed happy enough since it smelt of home. But sometimes I had to take a taxi, and the driver would become suspicious if the briefcase suddenly began to bulge or emit plaintive cries.

But the waiting room was worse, with the odour of strange animals, mainly dogs, pervading the atmosphere. Our delicate cat scrabbled and meowed, until I allowed him to peep out, yet the little bells on his neck collar would clatter with terror when his jewel-like blue eyes caught a glimpse of some massive ailing canine. I became friendly with the other habitués of the waiting room, often elderly people for whom the companionship of their cat or dog was crucial. 'Ah, Professor Montague,' one old lady sighed, 'they don't live long enough. And I don't think I'll have the courage to get another one.'

CALYPSO

A few years after the tumult of May '68, the political atmosphere
had grown calmer in both France and America, though not necessarily for positive reasons. In America, for instance, an
exhausted bitterness was thickening amongst the anti-Vietnam
protesters after Nixon and Kissinger – that arrogant and evil
duo – had decided, outrageously, to bomb Cambodia without
consulting Congress. It seemed that the Leftists of Berkeley and
New York were almost giving up. In my native Ulster, however,
the political cauldron was on the boil, while in Paris my personal life was in a state of upheaval.

The decision to leave my companion of nearly two decades,
to quit the serene sanctuary of the Rue Daguerre, and to
exchange Paris for Cork, was of course not easy. And under-
standably, Madeleine did not wish for our quite lively and
civilised life to be disrupted. She was, after all, a French woman
of good background who believed that marriages can, and
should, survive change, strife and even sexual adventures, as
long as both partners conduct their affairs (in both senses of the
word) with tact and courtesy. Indeed, Jean-Paul and Simone
lived just round the corner, and Madeleine had always admired
The Second Sex. An urbane and practical French lady, she did not
see why we could not model our own arrangement on that of
those two great intellectuals. But I feared to become like
Valmont in *Les Liaisons Dangereuses*, and in fact the posthumous
letters of de Beauvoir and Sartre would show a similar pattern
of collusion between a couple in allowing or even fostering
infidelity.

I realise that throughout this account I have repeated a

refrain: why? Why did I choose not to return to ever-vernal Berkeley? Why did I resist enticements that so many in my place would have accepted with delight? What, after all, was I afraid of? I thought again of Odysseus, though this time not in terms of Circe, but Calypso. Odysseus and his sailors, wooed by Calypso and her minions, are engulfed by so much sensual pleasure that they fall into a kind of dream or stupor. Opening their eyes after sleeping on perfumed couches, the men believe they have spent one night on Calypso's island, only to learn that they have been there, caught in a blissful spell, for ten years.

For ten years I had lived on and off in Paris, Berkeley and Dublin, in a comradely marriage that allowed both parties a good deal of freedom. I am also aware, though, that the second refrain which sounds throughout this chronicle has to do with the limits of freedom. During the 1960s, I had experienced both the French practice of discreet affairs, and the adventurous though curiously wholesome attitudes of 'Guru' Snyder and his erotic disciples. And I had begun to ask myself: what are the responsibilities attendant on freedom? And when does freedom become licence?

Thanks to the arrangement between Madeleine and myself, I had been able to pursue 'my craft or sullen art' without much worry, economic or otherwise. Yet I did not wish to travel from youth to old age without shouldering the responsibilities of adulthood. I feared the fate of Odysseus and his men, so stupefied with pampering that they fail to realise that time is passing. An endless supply of young women – a serial sensuality – could, I suspected, be as sapping as abstinence. And while Berkeley had sometimes seemed to me a Spenserian 'Bower of Bliss', one could perhaps drown in honey. Stendhal's theory, as embodied in his swashbuckling heroes, was that love is by nature deliciously transitory, and that affairs should begin and end with little fuss or regret. Clearly, I was no Stendhalian. Besides, Ireland was changing, and seemed to beckon me back.

8

PATRIOTIC SUITE

> Again, that note! A weaving
> melancholy, like a bird crossing
> moorland . . .

The argument about Seán Ó Riada's central achievement continues. We are all inclined to glamorise those who die young, and Seán has come to embody the Irish equivalent of Chopin's legend. That he was musically gifted, in diverse ways, is beyond doubt, but did the diversity deflect the intensity? Or was he the first major Irish composer?

Of his earliest musical self, Ó Riada the jazz pianist, we have no recordings, but we can presume that it gave him that sense of improvisation which he brought to bear on Irish traditional music. He was an enthusiastic jazz musician; even now, when I attend the Cork Jazz Festival, older players ask me, 'What happened to John Reidy? He was in at the beginnings of jazz in this town, playing with that fine trombonist Bobby Lamb, and the O'Callaghan Band from Mallow.' Seán's jazz phase was over by the time we met, though he would occasionally speak wistfully of George Shearing, or ask me about the piano playing of Dave Brubeck, whom I had met in California.

Seán Ó Riada had recognisable genius, that peculiar radiance or emotional electricity which attracts, or sometimes repels, people. I stress the personal impact, although that quality is not always necessary for the production of great work. For instance, the dispute as to whether Patrick Kavanagh or Austin Clarke bore the mantle of champion Irish poet is irrelevant because it ignores that difference. Austin the man could be charming and dignified, as well as melancholy and mordant, but he did not have the immediate effect on people, the dramatic presence, of Patrick Kavanagh, to which one could not remain indifferent: Patrick was seismic.

A reason for Kavanagh's unease with Brendan Behan was that Brendan also had it, albeit in a raw or primary state. For a few years, when he was working well and at ease with his wife Beatrice, that little Northside Napoleon shone with happy energy. But it broke him as well, when the public act supplanted the private achievement. Beckett also had the radium of genius, but wisely husbanded it for the work, avoiding first nights of even his own plays.

But what if you are part of the performing arts in an even more intense way than a dramatist? I knew Seán Ó Riada as a name before I met him; descriptions of wild evenings at Galloping Green when the carpet was rolled back for dancing, and the music and drink flowed, did not appeal to me. I had my own needs and scenes to deal with, and Garech Browne had already got me deep enough into traditional Irish music – too deep, I sometimes thought, as another singer's head went back and some unearthly wail smote the night.

So I was nearly hostile when I met Seán, regarding him, perhaps, as a parody of aspects of myself, a russet-headed apostle of the Gael – which, as far as I was concerned, was only part of the message. But one night, in Garech's first little flat, Seán sat up with me and proceeded to analyse my first sizeable book of poems, *Poisoned Lands*, with a minatory exactness. He told me what he thought was wrong and right about it, and I had to agree with most of his judgement, for, apart from the personal interest, I realised that I was in the presence of a formidable intellect. He then moved on to our mutual friend, Thomas Kinsella, with the same merciless accuracy. Again I listened, only occasionally dissenting. There was edge, but no malice.

I was conquered, as I suppose I was meant to be. That carefully prepared scene set the tone for most of our subsequent meetings, a heady mixture of affectionate competition, irritation and amusement. But I still wonder, to this day, what he wanted from me, for I had been shamed out of my Donegal Irish at University College Dublin, and had grown wary of the lure of the Gaelic tradition and its dangerously romantic association with nationalist politics. While I might have affection for that amiable Celtic eccentric, Garech Browne, who brought me into the Pipers Club, and even though I conspired to found Claddagh Records with him, that was more than enough musical patriotism for me.

But producing records, and dealing with artists and performers, gave me some further insight into Seán. He was an impresario of genius, appreciating the talent of relatively unsophisticated musicians, and gathering them together to create a folk orchestra of astonishing power, Ceoltori Chulainn. Although his father, as I remember, played the fiddle, Seán was not a traditional musician by nurture, and his efforts in that direction were a kind of delighted exploration, coinciding with the decision to change his name from John Reidy to Seán Ó Riada. But he was finally disappointed by it, and disbanded Ceoltori Chulainn in a famous radio interview, which left us all stunned. What he was saying, I now think, was that traditional music is naturally conservative, and could be pushed only so far without betrayal or distortion. Yet he had already done a great deal for it, giving status to musicians who had been forgotten, pushed aside after Ireland changed languages, and showing the way to groups like The Chieftains. It was left to them, and later groups, to carry

Irish traditional music into the wider world, and make a dialogue with other kinds of music, even pop, and other instruments, although Seán should be credited with the reintroduction of the bodhrán into Irish group playing.

He also reinterpreted Irish traditional music through his classical training, with startling results far beyond any previous arrangements of Irish airs by composers like Charles Villiers Stanford or Hamilton Harty. Because he was musically amphibious, moving fluidly between traditional and classical, he was able to give his film score *Mise Eire* a symphonic structure. It was a folk symphony, to be sure, like Sibelius' use of the Kalevala legends in *Finlandia*. But it sent a thrill of astonished pride through the nation to hear one of our oldest tunes, '*Roisín Dubh*' ('My Little Dark Rose'), surging lavishly out through a full orchestra, or the extremely modern, jagged tinkle of chords which mourns the execution of the rebel leaders of 1916. In 'Patriotic Suite', I would describe how 'Symbolic depth charge of music/ Releases a national dream . . . '.

But once again Seán abandoned a successful trajectory; the sequel to *Mise Eire*, *An Tine Beo*, is much less inventive. It was as though he wearied too quickly, once a challenge had been met; Seán had a low boredom threshold. At one point he had a column in the *Irish Times* which displayed his wide reading in several languages, but which also had the haphazard glitter of a magpie's nest, full of intriguing but disparate information. His more direct attacks on the symphonic form, in his *Nomoi*, were very ingenious but, unfortunately, we have only one recording of one of them, *Nomos No. One*, produced by Claddagh Records. Composed when Ó Riada was in his early twenties, it is a fine, dramatic piece for such a young man, with some of the theatrical flourish of *Mise Eire*. The hour-long *Nomos No. Two* is far more ambitious, but probably never achieved its final form because Seán died before he could perfect it.

Whenever I saw him, he was usually convalescing from some public performance, and fun and games were the order of the night, especially in the big salon at Woodtown Manor, with the lights of Dublin flickering in the distance. It was an attitude I sympathised with: I agreed with Goldsmith's remark that what one wants after a day's creative labour is relaxation, 'viva voce over the bottle'. But Seán's forms of relaxation were outrageously various, even frantic. While he and Paddy Moloney were tweeting on tin whistles, he would pause to bicker with an Irish sculptor in low German, and speak to me in fluent argot at the same time. The French poet Claude Esteban, who had come over with me to Ireland, staggered back from an exchange with Seán: '*Mais, qui est cet homme?*' he cried, hand to his head. '*Il est trop intelligent!*'

Around this time, with some pain and bewilderment, I began to realise that Seán was drinking far too much. It was hard to detect, because he had that dubious advantage, a good head for it; he rarely went though the character change induced by heavy drinking, the sudden rearing nastiness of Behan or others of my friends in the shark tank of McDaids. But there were many clues, if I had had the gumption to read them. He did not savour the slow pint, nor did he go for the sting of whiskey, preferring the odourless white lightning of vodka sweetened by tonic. He also liked brandy, but drowned in ginger ale. And finally there was the poteen which flowed in the West Cork Gaeltacht; smothered in milk or sweetened with honey, it was still lethal, and certainly contributed to his early death. I had tasted it myself when all his musical friends assembled at his home in Coolea for the west Cork practice of the 'Stations', or Mass in the home. Seán greeted me at the door with a tumbler of poteen so raw and strong, it literally drove me, staggering, through the house, to retch in the garden. As a daily tipple, it would have been disastrous.

Seán was a stylish man, partly eighteenth-century, a style acknowledged in his *Ceol na Uasal,* or 'Music of the Nobles', with its homage to Carolan. But the style began to falter in puzzling ways. We had stayed at Woodtown one night, and he came to see me as I was rising just after dawn. Gazing down at the tranquil autumn drive, I unburdened myself of a few painful confidences, the kind of things one tells a trusted friend. He listened with the sympathy and understanding I had hoped for, except that his reaction was more far violent than mine. 'If someone did that to me,' he said chillingly, 'I would have to think of killing them.' The confidence I had vouchsafed him was cause, I thought, for regret and sorrow; vengeance of the kind he described would never have occurred to me, and I was shocked by this glimpse of something dark, even paranoid, in his psyche, which would emerge later when there was trouble in the North.

But to the point: privacy seems to me one of the privileges of close friendship. I was horrified when, some months later, the story floated back to me, in a garbled version. I had to face the fact that Seán had told my halting, raw confidences to someone who did not seem to appreciate them as anything but sensational disclosures, titillating gossip.

Yet I kept my counsel because Garech and I, as directors of Claddagh Records, were moving towards the climax of our creative relationship with Seán. We had long wanted to present him as a formidable composer in his own right – not merely the most adept arranger of Irish music – and Garech was finally prepared to put his money where his mouth was. His generosity was equal to his tenacity: he met all Seán's grandiose conditions for the production of *Nomos No. One,* his Hölderlin Songs and settings to music of poems by Kinsella, Heaney and myself, in a record called *Vertical Man,* recorded in London. Feeling let down by our national orchestra, Seán insisted on the one-hundred-strong

London Symphony Orchestra, and on flying the celebrated Carlo Franci from Rome to London to conduct – expensive demands which Garech fulfilled without protest.

The job was done with professional alacrity, with a happy Seán looking on. Afterwards, there was a little recording time left over, so Paddy Moloney produced his tin whistle, and tootled away with the entire London Symphony Orchestra backing him. Garech could never hope to get his money back, but memories like Paddy playing Irish airs with the LSO swelling behind him are the reward for such ventures.

Seán was biased against our national orchestra probably because he felt neglected as a composer whose own work was seldom performed. Charles Acton, music critic of the *Irish Times*, said: 'RTÉ offered [Seán] neither deadlines nor the encouragement of repeats. I have become firmly convinced that, tricky and difficult as he undoubtedly was . . . RTÉ's music department during his last decade is primarily responsible for his pitifully small output.' We at Claddagh were trying to rectify that, but, alas, it was nearly too late.

Seán's grievance against the national orchestra was so great that, when he was drinking, he would declare that what we needed was a national folk orchestra, with the best of Irish musicians, instead of a pompous 'national' orchestra trying – and doubtless failing – to equal the 'Philharmonics' and 'Symphonys' of larger European and American cities. About the same time, I was friendly with the new head of RTÉ, that old IRA-gunman-turned-commissar Todd Andrews, who read poetry with intensity. He also had a biting Dublin wit: asked about the difference between his new job as director of RTÉ and his old job as head of the national transport system, he declared: 'RTÉ carries more passengers.' Coincidentally, he was concerned about the cost of the orchestra, the most expensive item in RTÉ's budget, and was quite prepared, old hatchet man that he was, to bear the blame for chopping it away, as he had the Harcourt Street railway line, beloved of Beckett. So it seemed to me that this was the right moment for Seán to strike, and that Todd would be ready to place him in charge of reorganising our national musical programme. I arranged a meeting and, to my dismay, Seán turned up drunk, rambling to Todd about the West Cork Brigade in a bleary attempt to prove his nationalist credentials. And when Seán was questioned brusquely about the orchestra, he backed down entirely, saying that every country had to have one.

Tom Kinsella, myself and Seán Lucy have all written poems about Seán Ó Riada – showing that a male can be a muse as well. It was a generational thing, of course: we were dazzled by the arc of his genius, and then stunned to sorrow by the signs of his decline, before his early death. Of course we were partly weeping for ourselves; after we had shouldered the coffin together at his funeral in Coolea in County Cork, Kinsella cried out in the fierceness of grief: 'The gobshite!' To hear the strains of his own Mass, at his own funeral, was a moving and an unnerving experience; under the gloss of modernity, Seán had a simple, old-fashioned faith. Beyond the ordeal of dying, I think that he was largely unafraid of death itself, in a way that would seem alien and perhaps innocent in our secular, or at least agnostic, age. But it did seem true of Seán, that he believed, quietly though fiercely, in the tenets of his Catholic religion, and truly wished for his soul to be liberated into that wider world described in his favourite medieval Irish poem, 'Under Sorrow's Sign'. (I had asked him to choose a poem that we might translate together, and he selected this remarkably gloomy one. The poem compares the soul to a small child born in prison, longing for the great world beyond the harsh confines of what we call 'life'.)

People are sometimes apologetically curious about the background to 'Ó Riada's Farewell' – both his last record and the title of my elegy for him. When Seán began to sense that he was dying, he called Garech Browne, and asked if he could record Irish tunes on the eighteenth-century harpsichord that Garech had acquired. Mystified, Garech agreed, especially since the silence at Luggala, his Wicklow estate, had already been used for the recording of *John Field Nocturnes*. The ancient harpsichord features on the record cover, its burnished wood shining like a coffin lid:

> clatter of harpsichord
> the music leaping
> like a long candle flame
> to light ancestral faces

I incorporate that imagery into my poem, the central drama of which derives from a furious argument between myself and Seán shortly before he died. The story of that argument might entail a breach of privacy of the kind I have chastised him for, but I will try to tell it tactfully. At this point in my marriage, long separations – Madeleine in Paris, myself in Dublin or Berkeley – had spawned a series of light affairs on both sides, which had almost begun to seem normal, although they were probably a harbinger of the marriage's demise. The year of Seán's death, I had become involved with that Californian girl, an exchange student at Trinity, whom I have already described as rollicking around with us in Garech's coach. This was a lighter, less troubling echo of my dark Berkeley affair, but Seán had decided that the young woman was, if not actually evil, then in some sense 'bad' for me, being only a vehicle for desire. He might have had a point, but who can say where lust ends and love begins? Infatuation can yield to love, or at least to genuine affection, and I have tried not to forget those whom I have touched or who have touched me, even if only briefly. And perhaps I detected in Seán's stern attitude a little of his old-fashioned Catholic self, a deep unease in the new sixties world of casual, guilt-free sex.

The girl in question was indeed a product of the sixties: by no means immoral, but naively at ease in the new climate of free love. Only she had formed an attachment to myself and not Seán, so that a deep though probably unconscious jealousy might also have influenced his baleful attitude towards her. Anyway, their distrust was mutual. She did not speak of it but seemed deeply afraid of him, and with reason. She and I had spent a cluttered, drunken evening with Seán, in which he had given a most unimpressive display of his magic powers. I do not use the word 'magic' flippantly or facetiously, because of the mysterious connection between certain kinds of art and magic. But I am also chary of any artist misusing the powers placed so briefly in his custody: the shaman or healer in the artist should foster the art, not take over the driving seat.

But Seán seemed to be wilfully letting this happen, a parody of the saint who must prove his point with miracles. Later that night, when the two of us were alone together by the fireside, our customary friendly banter turned sour. He told me I was in danger, and I responded that he was in worse: a harsh judgement that he accepted almost humbly. But suddenly he swerved back to his dark obsession with this girl, whom he insisted on identifying with death, going so far as to prophecy her barrenness and early demise. Worse, when the young woman joined us by the fire, he insisted on telling it to her face, while she wept silently.

> A door opens,
> and she steps into the room,
> smothered in a black gown,
> harsh black hair falling to her knees,
> a pallid tearstained face.
>
> How pretty you look,
> Miss Death!

The girl would in fact fall ill years later, long after she had resumed her life in California. I believe that she was probably a victim of that 1960s sexual phenomenon, the Pill. In the 'swinging sixties' we did not seem to know or care enough about the possible side effects of all the hormones that countless women were taking every day. Many of those women, including my Californian friend, would be stricken with cancer or other diseases when they were still relatively young. In the 1960s, AIDS had yet to afflict us, and we thought we were free, but the Pill was compromising women's health in ways that would only become clear later.

That night in Woodtown, I had no choice but to do what I had been taught as a child by those who cherished the old earth magic, and that I had relearnt from other poets – how to 'sett the wards'. I placed a walled circle around myself and her so that any harm would rebound from it. Today she has overcome her illness and is alive, while he, alas, is not, but I do not think my ritual of protection had much to do with it. It was Seán who had fallen in love with death, his powers betrayed and drained, due partly (or so it seemed to me) to his capricious trafficking in magic, and partly by the fervour of his nationalist mission. Obsessions fed, of course, by his lack of recognition as a composer, instead of merely a conductor or arranger. And through it all, the haze of spirit-sapping alcohol.

An example of the caprice was his telling myself and Garech, in a hotel bar, that he could make a man stumble; sure enough, the man he had indicated almost fell there and then. An example of his nationalist zeal was his telling me, on our next meeting, that, since he had seen me last, he had 'killed his man' in Belfast. Since I was from the North, and had some sense of how the IRA operated, I recognised a common alcohol-fuelled fantasy: no volunteer on active service would babble in such a fashion. Finally, an example of how alcohol was corroding his mind was given by his last lady friend, who described coming to his room in the Shelbourne Hotel and finding him lying fully clothed on the bed. 'Don't turn on the light,' he admonished, 'I am covered in blood.'

*

Few men have had as direct an effect on my life as Seán Ó Riada. The encounters I describe were mainly fruitful, for us both, I hope, although, as I have said, his nationalism troubled me, since it was so fervently idealistic – more an aisling or vision, than reality. But I am pleased that I wrote a poem for Seán during his lifetime. 'Patriotic Suite' is meant to be a bitter-sweet commentary on the contrast between the ideals of 1916, and the reality of our little nation state of 1966, a question mark after *Mise Eire*. I knew that Seán cultivated being a poor correspondent as one of his affectations. And perhaps travel, work, and especially drink are not conducive to answering letters. But I was still hurt when he did not write to acknowledge my poem, although word was passed along that he was pleased.

The news came through Seán Lucy, Corkman, poet and professor, who was assembling his *Anthology of Irish Love Poems*. I was sceptical about Lucy, with that too-easy, lofty disparagement which is, or was, part of Dublin life, and which I have tried to overcome. Ó Riada would have none of such arrogant Dublin disdain: 'There's someone there,' he assured me, 'you'll understand him yet.' I dismissed it as provincial loyalty, but he did seem more convinced than defiant in his praise of Lucy. At Seán's funeral, Lucy helped us shoulder the coffin, and I talked with him afterwards. Ó Riada's wife Ruth glimpsed me as I entered the wakehouse. 'Seán told me a lot about you,' she said, and added firmly, 'It's time for you to come home.'

Three months later I was teaching at University College Cork, with Seán Lucy as my friend and colleague. And now, here

I am, working on this salute to Seán Ó Riada with my novelist wife Elizabeth in our renovated west Cork farmhouse, surrounded by rugged hills that remind me of Tyrone. To say that I feel tele-guided would be to exaggerate, but Ó Riada did wish that I should become a friend of his earlier friend, another Seán, and that in some sense I should take up the slack of his achievement in music by bringing encouragement in a different sphere. With his widow's admonition that I should 'come home', I believe, or deceive myself, that Seán Ó Riada still wishes me well, mockingly urging me on, and is still a comrade across the great void or divide. One may reflect how the worldly failure of a poet like Kavanagh, who wrote with passion and loneliness about rural Ireland, has been redeemed by the worldly success of Seamus Heaney, also a chronicler of rural Ireland, though in a later time. But I imagine Seán's blessing not in the manner of failure being transformed into success, but as an act of transference, and indeed affection.

*

Seán had indeed done the state great service, and some knew it. But for an artist to be most renowned for his secondary, if more spectacular, gift can be dangerous. Mahler may have made his living as a conductor, but he knew he was a composer first, and pressed on with his work, despite pain and bitter disappointment. We cannot say with certainty whether Seán could have been a truly great composer. A poet can weather censorship and prison camps, his truth enduring by word of mouth – that carrier pigeon of the spirit. But a composer needs all those lavish accoutrements, needs an orchestra and performances, needs more than just one concerned critic. *Nomos No. Two* was performed only once during his lifetime, and once more after his death. There is a long movement portentous with sorrow, and that weird finale, where he uses the eclectic devices of *The Waste*

Land, with snatches of Mozart and Beethoven, those splendid clichés of Western music. The central theme is devastating, declaring that the composer would prefer not to have been born, and that Western music is at the end of its tether. This was thrilling to listen to, as I thought when I finally heard that second posthumous performance, but, caught in the welter of pain between grief at his death and the events of Bloody Sunday, how could one have anything but a highly emotional and uncritical response to such music?

There was something devil-may-care, almost flashy, about Seán. People succumbed to a vivid charm that drew out the best in themselves. Kinsella and I have rarely had such good meetings as when Ó Riada was there, a taunting catalyst. 'Art has nothing to do with life,' he provocatively pronounces, and, as Kinsella agrees, I smash the stem of my glass. A minute later, we collapse into helpless giggles, even the seemingly sombre Tom.

It is savagely ironical that we were recording Seán's first major work, *Nomos No. One*, when he was dying, and when he had left classical music aside. Would it have been better if he had reversed the process, deepening his gift by moving from folk to classical, instead of the other way round? I believe that would have been more or less impossible, since he would have had to reopen the ears of middle-class concert-going audiences, who were not his kind of people anyway. And Western music was then in a cul-de-sac, with Boulez as the Mondrian or Mallarmé of the concert halls, and a poor lad from Ireland (which had never had the structure – the halls and great houses – to support a tradition of classical music) would not have had a chance. He would have brought the ardour of youth to an art which had grown exhausted, overburdened by the old traditions, with composers in crisis.

Seán affected to find a connection between serial music and the most pure *sean nos*, or old style of Irish unaccompanied singing, which he also associated with the wailing music of the Arabs, and even Indian music, the Celtic aesthetic being circular, from the Book of Kells to *Finnegans Wake*. But I am only partly convinced. In his later years, while he might have composed less, he helped to revive a dying community by giving it a moving, living choral voice that dramatised the Indian-reservation plight of the Gaeltacht, and he wrote a beautiful and simple Mass in Irish for them. Not what he would have dreamt of in his more grandiose moments, but not bad. And of course, largely because of him, Irish music now has a world-wide audience, with even the avant-garde doing fairly well. If the Irish composer now has a better life, it is partly because of Seán Ó Riada's death.

> Roving unsatisfied ghost,
> old friend, lean closer;
> leave us your skills:
> lie still in the quiet
> of your chosen earth.

9

STARTING AGAIN

OR WHAT ARE YOU DOING HERE?

In January 1972, I received a phone call in my exile's studio in Paris, from Seán Lucy, to say that there was a vacancy for me in the English Department of University College Cork, which might become permanent. I hesitated: it was the lowliest academic position I had ever been offered: temporary assistant lecturer! After a fairly respectable academic and literary career, I would be starting at the bottom again, in my early forties.

So why, when I had refused a tempting post in balmy Berkeley, would I accept to go back to Ireland's second city, a southern marshland that I barely knew (*Corcaigh* in Irish does indeed mean 'marsh' or 'fen'), and which Dubliners tended to dismiss with a condescending joke? But I had some sense of the long literary history of Cork, from Spenser's Kilcolman – where he had laboured at *The Faerie Queene*, bringing cantos down regularly to his friend Raleigh at Myrtle Lodge in the fishing town of Youghal – to the last Gaelic poets of eighteenth-century Munster, celebrated by Daniel Corkery in his *Hidden Ireland*.

Besides, I had finally met Seán Lucy at the Yeats Summer School in Sligo, and liked his courteous style, as well as being impressed by his romantic, almost histrionic lecturing skills, all swirling gown and elegant gesture. And of course Seán Ó Riada had made UCC sound like some kind of ideal place, vibrant and progressive, with students and professors collaborating in a lengthy teach-in, along the models of Berkeley and Vincennes. Astonishingly, I was receiving the impression that little Cork University was more politically active and defiant than UCD or Trinity, and Ó Riada was also enthusiastic about how the university tried to blend the Irish and English traditions – an ambition reflected in my growing Faber anthology.

But my old left-wing journalist friend Claud Cockburn, who lived with his wife Patricia beside Raleigh's Myrtle Lodge, extolled not Cork city but remote *east* Cork as the ideal lopsided angle from which to regard the universe. And sitting in Cork Airport, I saw, opposite me, a tall woman, as noble-looking as a finely bred horse: it was Elizabeth Bowen, who traced her family back to fertile *north* Cork, not far from Spenser's fastness. My glimpse of that fiercely intelligent face recalled Henry James' account of his first sight of George Eliot, equine and handsome like the woman before me now. He felt that he should kneel in homage to her, because she shone with such creative power. Elizabeth Bowen looked up impatiently from her book once or twice, and I could have gone over. Yet everyone said that she was massively shy, one of the few women with a stammer; so I hesitated to approach her, imagining the pair of us faltering and stumbling and missing our planes as we stammered in chorus.

I was driven also by a powerful sense that I had to be back in Ireland, now that I had finished *The Rough Field*, which was a kind of prophecy or premonition: old moulds were indeed breaking in the North. I sat with Evelyn in the Ormonde Hotel in Dublin as images of Bloody Sunday flashed on the television above the bar, silencing even the hardest drinkers. Small grainy figures, some adolescents, being mowed down; troops in full camouflage gear running with guns at the ready; a priest bravely facing them, waving a small white handkerchief. Some of those

images, taken by an Italian television film company, were to
strangely disappear afterwards, but in that short time, on an
otherwise ordinary Sunday, they were seared into the national
consciousness: an apparently peaceful civil-rights protest of the
kind I had experienced in Berkeley, and afterwards in Paris, as
well as in my native Tyrone, being deliberately gunned down
before our eyes.

Ironically, despite Seán Ó Riada's description of fiery campus activism, Cork was less politically involved in the Northern
problem than any other part of Ireland, partly, though not whol-
ly, due to geography. Of course Cork is as physically remote
from the North as is possible on our small island. But there was
a psychological factor in its political indifference as well. Despite
being called 'Rebel Cork', this diverse southern county, the
largest in the Republic, had achieved most of the political auton-
omy it sought; so that one could almost accuse Cork of being
complacent. (When Brian Friel's *Translations* was performed in
the Cork Opera House, Stephen Rea asked me to explain to a
baffled Friel why the sombre last act, which had been applaud-
ed in Dublin and Broadway, was received here in uncompre-
hending silence. 'They like to believe that they have never been
defeated,' I said to Brian. And more recently, I was astonished,
after a hurling victory, to meet no jubilation in any of the Cork
pubs. 'Why are you not celebrating?' I asked a barman, who
laughed, 'Yerrah, here we're used to winning.')

This curious complacency would have an interesting effect
on my attempt at a second relationship. Whatever about the private lives of the citizens of Cork, which seemed as complicated
as any other place, it was all kept genteelly covert, with everyone
aspiring to be respectable – unlike the vigorous, working-class
culture of Dublin, celebrated from O'Casey to Behan. Indeed,
there was no recent play or novel to give me a glimpse of how
the Corkonians were disporting themselves; it was as though

they were so afraid of what their neighbours might think, it had frozen the ink in their pens. For someone to live openly in what the Church called sin seemed inconceivable in Cork, and our neighbours – simply, perhaps generously – assumed that myself and my new partner were married. But this old-fashioned attitude served us well, because when one is embarking on a new life, one needs a home or nest, a domestic sanctuary.

And through the Cork Arts Society on Lavitt's Quay, we were welcomed by a small group of Cork people connected with the arts: the sculptor Seamus Murphy, his wife Mairead, and journalists like Geraldine Neeson and Robert O'Donoghue. I remember, as a kind of revelation, Seamus showing me how to walk home across the town at night from his house, always keeping 'the much-divided flood' of Spenser's Lee in view. I came to feel an affection for the terraced streets of this hilly city, an Irish Bergen or San Francisco, from which I could gaze down at the flashing harbour lights, reminding me that Cork was still a bustling port. I resolved to try to find an eyrie, from which I could view this urban energy, from the trains drawing in and out of Glanmire Station, to the maritime gleam and clang of the dockyards, and the occasional plane climbing from the then-little airport.

I was trying, as always, to link my worlds; so we drove up through the middle of Ireland, to join a civil-rights march in Enniskillen, and of course to visit my mother in hospital. She was dying, and I did not wish to vex her with the changes in my life, especially since she was in an almost hallucinatory state as it was, declaring that the pleasant, probably Protestant, nurses, treading quietly around and offering us cups of tea, were really rabid Orangewomen. This was at sharp variance with the denial cooked up by the staunch Protestant lady in charge of our bed and breakfast, who proclaimed that the helicopters hovering in the calm sky above the march were conveying tourists into Fermanagh's lovely lake district – in chill February.

It was important, I thought, to introduce my new companion to my brothers. My elder brother, a country doctor, had been explaining to me that he had discovered that our great-grandfather Carney had been a Fenian and, like our rebel uncles, had spent time in prison. This seemed a good moment to announce another family scandal: I was going to get the first divorce and remarriage in Montague–Carney history. (After all, even though my parents had been long separated – he in Brooklyn, she back in Tyrone – my mother could not abide the taboo word 'divorce'. She almost preferred 'cancer', which she would utter in hushed tones during gossip sessions in her murky Fintona pub.)

Now my elder brother's jaw dropped, but he quickly righted himself with a flash of humour. 'Well, Johnny, we can live this down, too.' My middle brother, perhaps because he was a lawyer and all too sensitive to the complexities of local custom, was less sure. 'There's no divorce you could get that we'd be able to recognise,' he said worriedly. 'Why don't you try the Vatican?' My elder brother's wife was plying us with a potent punch, from a bottle of poteen that a grateful patient had given him. Frances prepared it with cloves and hot water under my seasoned instruction; that festive smell, like that of a Christmas ham, failed to dissolve the tensions completely, but it did help.

My relief at managing to keep my family informed of this profound change in my life turned to dismay when we returned to Cork, and Evelyn suddenly fell ill. A young doctor, called O'Sullivan, appeared, and peered into her eyes, diagnosing severe hepatitis. Strangely, he did not reappear. It became obvious that there was no way she could be treated properly in a ramshackle B&B, meant for transients, with only a hurried fried breakfast available in the morning, and with no facilities for a long stay, especially if one were an invalid. And I was caught between a desire to look after my ill partner, and the need to devote myself more or less full-time to establishing myself at the university, for the future of us both. So we decided that she should fly back to Paris and her mother's care, while I ploughed my lonely furrow at UCC. On the afternoon of the day she left, I had to speak to the assembled Munster Teachers of English, as the new literary light come to illuminate their province. But I was so distraught after this reversal that I gulped and gaped like a dying fish, especially as I tried to read love poems which – ironically, given the timing – was a special request of theirs. The teachers were extremely kind, but it was not the sort of debut I would have wished for in my new home province.

And also, despite the encomia of my two Seáns, Ó Riada and Lucy, lecturing at UCC seemed an uphill task. For Cork was still an old-fashioned university, with the English department using large, gloomy lecture halls to recycle material that would then reappear on exam papers. This was splendid for Seán Lucy, who knew the students' backgrounds and could work variations on the formulae. But brimming with the zeal of Berkeley and Vincennes, I could not give standard lectures, to be taken down diligently by a battalion of docile pens, and then learnt by heart for the examinations. I had been exposed to a new way of teaching, with an attempt at exchange between student and teacher, and where it was assumed that the classroom was a forum for dialogue and challenge, and the teacher was not a separate and sacred being, despite his solemn gown. (Which in any case I decided not to wear.)

Something had to be done. I was teaching the first wave of the Romantics – Wordsworth et al – to a throng of earnest students, including two front lines of nuns, Nigerian Sisters in their starched blue habits, alongside less exotic Irish Sisters in standard-issue black and white. I knew all too well the kind of teaching they had endured in their convents and colleges, where Wordsworth would have meant 'a host of golden daffodils' and lonely clouds, and where they would have answered the teacher with the necessary platitudes about pantheism. Instead, looking out at their expectant faces and poised pens, I launched into a dramatic analysis of the private life of Wordsworth. There was this gaunt rustic orphan, this bony idealist, who had found himself caught up in the French Revolution and, kindled by the high emotion surrounding him, had plunged into a fiery love affair with a young Frenchwoman of good birth, with whom he had fathered a child. Both of whom he deserted: I read out the passionate, forlorn letters of Annette Vallon to her William, describing how much his baby daughter resembled him (especially the formidable nose). I was using shock tactics because I knew the ingrained piety of my audience.

Note-taking stopped as pens dropped from suddenly nerveless fingers: how could they write down such dangerously erotic material, which might make their notebooks explode? What had Wordsworth's youthful gallivanting to do with poetry? I swerved into a discourse on 'Nutting', as a poem of violation, the wanton pillage of a 'virgin nook', an interpretation that had also been broached by Harold Bloom. Wordsworth was beginning to look like the kind of man they had been brought up to disapprove of, a seducer and betrayer of women, whose lofty moral tone disguised the truth of his caddish behaviour in foreign parts; doubtless their mothers had cautioned them about men like that! Across the front of the class where the women sat, there was a collective intake of breath.

I went on to describe how that churl Wordsworth saved his skin by fleeing back to England, and the consoling arms of his sister Dorothy. I compared her wonderful prose account of daffodils to his all-too-well-known verses, and showed how, once again, he seemed to be living off the emotional strength of a woman. What was their real relationship? Dorothy adored him, and if he had been an insouciant lord like Byron, he might have known what to do about it, but there were limits to

Wordsworth's understanding of himself. There was no doubt that his sister loved him most deeply, a point I drove home to my aghast audience by reading out her letters at the time of his marriage, a ceremony she could not bear to attend. And there was also the ardent way she addressed him as 'Beloved'.

The large class was now silent: it was the silence of shock and dismay, as all the formal structure of English they had absorbed up to this point seemed to crash around their ears. They filed out without looking at me – all except for a few grinning miscreants whom I had already met in the bars around the university. Bars like the Western Star, where I had sat quietly writing beside the craggy presence of Moss Keane, the great Munster and Ireland rugby star, who smiled approval at my contemplative activity while we slowly sank our pints.

The class were so flabbergasted that they fell into my trap: they sent a deputation to my head of department, Professor Lucy, to complain about my unseemly lecture, an insult to faith and morals. Trying hard not to break into laughter, Seán blandly assured them that he was sure that Professor Montague would welcome an open debate – something they had never met in a lecture hall before.

The Physics Theatre was crowded; I noticed students from other years, contributing to a constant crackle, like a disturbed hive. I strode in with an armful of books, which I placed ostentatiously in front of me, as mental artillery: I had ransacked the rather old-fashioned university library, and even gone to the city libraries. And I had already organised a small fifth column, my poetic aspirants, who had planted themselves around the room. The students were hesitant at first, but soon warmed to the fray; even some of the timid nuns spoke up from within their wimples. Presently even the most cowed and prim were arguing animatedly, talking amongst themselves as well as to their professor, a sign that they were truly engaged in that most un-Irish of activities: trying to think for themselves. As the debate about the sexual implications of 'Nutting' became heated, the lights went off in the large hall. 'You see what you've done,' I cried. 'You have left us all in the dark. Clearly you have incurred the wrath of the Gods of Poetry.' They did not know that I was controlling the main light switch, under the massive bench, with my knee. (That, and maintaining that 'pantheism' could also mean 'the worship of the satyr-god Pan, grinning through the groves', was the only really low trick I played.)

From then on, I was able to teach in a way that I had dreamt of, voyaging more deeply into the Romantics, from the dramatic intensity of *The Rime of the Ancient Mariner* to the sweetness of Keats and the ardour of Shelley. I was afire with my new-found loneliness, channelling the accumulated energies of my solitary sojourn in the gaunt attic room of my B&B into an almost messianic teaching zeal. Remembering Ginsberg, I chanted aloud Blake's *Proverbs of Heaven and Hell*, spreading my arms wide like wings at the end of class. 'Everything that lives is holy,' I sang in resonant, prophetic tones; this time the class clapped, as if to urge on their demented captain.

But the climax of our teaching adventure was when Seán Lucy joined me to break the news of the advent of modern poetry, beginning with our *Waste Land* duet, Seán sombre and priestly, while I handled the lowlife scenes in an approximation of a Cockney rasp. Our minds dovetailed splendidly, and I am nearly sure that that stern and brilliant actress Fiona Shaw (then our student, Fifi Wilson) heard this academic tour de force. At least I would like to believe that her ensuing one-woman *Waste Land* was to some degree inspired by our antic virtuosity.

By chance or coincidence, some of my students were the best I'd ever had: they were literally mad about poetry, over and above the dictates of examinations. There was a lean young poet whose long hair and romantically hollow cheeks evoked Don

Quixote or the Ancient Mariner. It was the last gasp of the hippie era, when students flaunted the wildest of gear, and Gregory O'Donoghue had ransacked the family wardrobe to make himself look like a descendant of James Clarence Mangan's 'Man in the Cloak'. A disciple of Berryman, he wrote nervous, taut poems that were as lean as himself, while his pal Maurice Riordan, from Lisgoold, County Cork, was working on Hart Crane, and composing layered, inlaid verses of his own.

Another student poet was a striking young woman, frail though intense, with pale skin and long auburn hair. She was clearly very bright, but labouring under some kind of cloud. Yet when I needed help, she came to my rescue. I was trying to draw the class into a close analysis of Blake's 'London', by asking them what could the poet possibly intend by such lines as 'How the youthful harlot's curse/ Blights with plague the marriage hearse'? The students looked mystified, but Nuala Ní Dhomnhaill's firm voice rang out clearly: 'Why, he means the pox, of course.'

The gifted Nuala was already publishing in *Innti*, the Irish-language literary magazine, which was edited by another young poet, Michael Davitt. Michael was an even more flamboyant figure than Gregory: he sported a black, wide-brimmed Spanish hat, which made him look like a Renaissance cleric. He was also immensely tall, with loads of curls. When I was asked to conduct a poetry workshop in John B. Keane's Listowel in 1973, I swept Michael and Gregory along, to represent both strands of Cork's bilingual literary tradition.

But the most welcoming presence to me, on the Cork Irish-language literary scene, was the curious, oblique figure of Seán Ó Riordáin. He spoke in his *Irish Times* column of my appearance in Cork in my big coat, or *cota mór*, and with my head of hair, *mo chuid gruaige*. As so often happens with truly shy people, he was considered haughty and unapproachable. But while our exchanges would begin slowly, he would warm to his subject matter: linguistics, or the low life of Cork, both of which he seemed to know a great deal about. And since I was living alone, I sometimes wandered at night along the curving streets and quays of what was still a harbour town. According to my friend Michael Scott, who helped design Cork's new Opera House, the city had been laced with canals in the eighteenth century, and when I walked along the Grand Parade I could nearly feel a ghostly flow beneath the cobbles. Indeed, Cork struck me as a marvellously watery city, with small waterfalls everywhere, and swans huddled under the lichened arches of the numerous bridges, as in Spenser's wonderful marriage poem.

And depending on what ship was in, I would be joined on my nightly ramblings by French, American, English or even Russian sailors. There were even a few late-night hostelries and nightclubs, and of course pubs that served drink in the very early morning, down by the docks. Another favourite watering place, where I would often gather with the young poets, was the Long Valley, in Winthrop Street. It was indeed long, and dark and narrow like the hold of a ship, an effect enhanced by the furniture, taken from the wreck of the SS *Celtic*, which had sunk at the mouth of Cork harbour. So our diminutive host, Humphrey Moynihan, would beckon us to the gleaming circle of the captain's table.

We often went to the Long Valley after a performance in our reading series. As soon as I had managed to settle down, after Easter, when Evelyn had recovered and returned, I began to invite my literary friends to discover Cork and stir the students still more. The first I asked was Seamus Heaney, who had moved to Dublin from Belfast at almost the same time as my own move from Paris to Cork. He came down for a few days with Marie, and we explored the city, as well as Kinsale, where Louis MacNeice's widow, Hedli, now lived.

I also asked over some of the elders I admired, beginning

with Hugh MacDiarmid, who was, by his own admission, 'Scotland's greatest poet'. I had long been amused by his solution to the problem of the public and the private; MacDiarmid might be a rabid Marxist and Scottish nationalist, flaunting his Anglophobia, but Christopher Murray Grieve (his real name) was mild and affable. Hugh responded warmly to the Cork audience ('the best I've ever had,' he would declare afterwards), requesting a dram to quench his thirst so that he could plunge into an encore. His poem on the Shetlands, 'Island Funeral', so thrilled one of my brightest students, Patrick Crotty, that he would become a scholar of contemporary Scottish poetry, writing his thesis on MacDiarmid.

And Robert Graves wrote from Majorca to say that he would be glad to revisit Ireland, especially the province of Munster, where his paternal family had come from. Silver-haired and large-hatted, he arrived at Cork Airport with his entourage, some of whom went to stay with the Lucys (Seán's mother had been one of Graves' poetic disciples), while others were billeted with us. Robert was now eighty, and his mind was slipping a little, but his presence was still potent, especially for the second wave of young student poets, whom I had begun to meet in friendly venues like the Long Valley. Two of them were actually from Waterford: Tom McCarthy, with his russet curls and warm smile, from the beautiful village of Cappoquin; and the dark, gauntly romantic Seán Dunne, with his burning eyes. Amongst the Cork-born poets were Gerry Murphy, whose droll poems recalled e. e. cummings, and the curly-headed Greg Delanty, who would write movingly about his working-class printer father. The passionately eloquent Theo Dorgan had a flair for aesthetic theory as well as poetry: Robert seemed to recognise a fellow devotee of the Muse, and they exchanged a ceremonial rose. Dublin wits, hearing of this Wordsworthian host of young southern poets, began to describe Cork as 'Bloomsbury on the Lee'.

It was not all plain sailing, of course. Occasionally I came up against a kind of second-city inferiority complex: an older professor, whom I had met at a literary conference abroad, stopped me in the street, demanding with incredulity: 'What are you doing here?' – a disconcerting welcome. A well-known tattle-tale, he regaled the locals with details of my supposed misbehaviour at overseas shindigs. (I was beginning to get used to such highly coloured stories as part of the necessity of one's legend, as when I heard of an all-night party in Kansas City where I had danced on the tables; I had never, alas, even been to that city. But it was harder to laugh off this kind of florid tale in my new home place.)

Another time, I foolishly asked a history professor his opinion of my use of Irish history in *The Rough Field*. 'If I wrote a book,' he said with a curl of the lip, 'I wouldn't go round asking people's opinion of it.' He would manage to publish only one small pamphlet, which might have been why my relative productivity provoked such rancour in this particular Corkman; anyway, his extraordinary malice would obstruct my career whenever possible.

Then there was the casual spite couched in banter, as when I was arranging for another contemporary to come to speak. I rang him from my office, but took his answer in the tutors' room, where our exchange was overheard. 'Was that So-and-So you were speaking to?' asked a tutor behind me, in the querulous, lilting tones of Cork. 'Is he coming down to visit us here?'

'Yes,' I answered amiably, unaware that I was walking into a trap. 'I think he'll probably stay a few days, and give a lecture as well as a reading.'

'That's grand,' answered the tutor with a complacent sneer. 'For he's a far better writer than ye.'

I retorted sharply, 'Well, by Christ, he's not coming down to see the likes of you!'

I was wrong, of course, even to bother to answer, but this kind of spiteful taunting still unnerves me. I presumed that one was meant to chuckle at such sallies, though clearly they bristled with hostility. Yet soon enough I learnt how to weather this Cork chorus of aggrieved doves (or so their accent, melodious yet petulant-sounding, made them seem), the other side of the coin of Cork hospitality. I found little of this mean-spiritedness amongst the older people. For instance, we were befriended by the sculptor Seamus Murphy, who had fashioned endearing fig-ures like little St Gobnait, patron saint of bees, who stands in the cemetery that bears her name, and where Seán Ó Riada is buried. He and his highly intelligent wife Mairead introduced us to the remote, romantic beauty of Roche's Point, at the mouth of Cork harbour. There we found a haven when Evelyn was pregnant with our first child, Oonagh. And we also began to explore west Cork, with its bohemian colony of potters and painters, who had settled in the traditionally colourful villages. They lived in brightly painted houses beside hedges aglow with scarlet fuchsia, bordering the wild Atlantic.

Lest I fall utterly in love with both the maritime city of Cork and the diversity of County Cork, I was given a pungent warn-ing. As I have explained, I had slowly become aware of the neg-ative aspects of my adopted home, a certain second-city defen-siveness, an occasional burst of sour envy from a colleague or acquaintance. But every place, like every person, has a complex character, and my impression of Cork was generally good. Except I did continue to wonder why her two fine native prose writers, Frank O'Connor and Seán O'Faolain, had chosen to quit the city in a way that seemed so final and extreme. I received an explanation from an elderly though still sharp O'Faolain, when I called on him once in Dublin. 'John,' he said sternly, 'don't ever trust them. I know the meanness of Cork. They'll give you that auld *plamás* to the eyebrows, but then they'll pull you down.

Their real intellectual level stops at a Munster Final. A visual artist might get by, but anyone who deals in words is dangerous, offends their bourgeois squeamishness.' And I remembered one of the newspaper-owning Crosbys coming into my quiet Cork local, Henchy's, and looking over my shoulder at an article I was writing. 'Is that piece about us?' he asked waspishly, narrowing his eyes at the biro in my hand. 'Don't knock Cork, or we'll tear you to pieces.'

But taken altogether, Cork seemed a good and generous setting in which to launch into a new life. There might be noises off stage in my native North, as when I went with Tom Kinsella to join the big protest march in Newry after Bloody Sunday, and when I stood, once more with Tom, as well as the former dean of Columbia University, Kevin O'Sullivan, while the angry crowds began to surge against the British Embassy in Dublin's Merrion Square. But all this felt far distant from Cork, with its motto that seemed like a talisman for my own new adventure: *Statio Bene, Fide Carinis.* Or 'A Good Harbour, Faithful to Ships'. There would be jagged rocks ahead, in both my private and public life, but for now it seemed I had found a haven.

> Lights in the harbour,
> An overnight fire, still
> Warm and glowing.
> After ten years, I find
> Myself back in Ireland,
> Watching from a window
> At dawn, the arc traced
> By a slowly ascending ship,
> A city flaring awake . . .

AFTERWORDS

I

The Private Life

Because this book is partly a meditation on sexual mores, I feel inclined to reflect further on my own private life in the turbulent 1960s. During that period, international travel was more prolonged than today, with many more stopovers, and I would fly to Berkeley via Dublin, New York or Chicago. And once, in 1966, while in Dublin en route to California, I decided to call on my friend Father Burke-Savage, who lived in the Jesuit house on Lower Leeson Street. (The neglected, sooty painting decorating the dining room of that house would turn out to be Caravaggio's *The Taking of Christ*, which now hangs in the National Gallery of Ireland.)

In the course of our chat, Father Burke-Savage offered to hear my Confession. At this point in my life I was something of a lapsed Catholic, though not all that lapsed, and so I consented. Only we struck a stone when the subject of marital fidelity arose.

'But don't you *wish* to be faithful?' the priest asked worriedly.

'No, Father. If I am to be honest, I must admit that I enjoy my liaisons. Sex is a path to knowledge, a way to know someone else in more than the Biblical sense, one of life's most exciting adventures, which I don't wish to give up, especially as there was so little pleasure in the Ireland I grew up in.'

Father Burke-Savage seemed genuinely upset. 'Then I can't grant you absolution, John,' he said sadly.

I think I was so adamant partly because it annoyed me to be lectured on the rights and wrongs of sex by a celibate. But I tell this story for another reason. I have said that the part of me which remained a pious Ulster Catholic, a chaste ex-altar boy, collided, in the 1960s, with both the French style of extramarital sex, and the free-love movement of that decade. While I liked the free-wheeling evenings in North Beach with Gary Snyder, I blanched at the thought of group sex, for which Gary derided me as an 'uptight, old-fashioned Irishman'. But where was that uptight, old-fashioned Irishman when Father Burke-Savage tried to persuade me to embrace constancy in marriage? If it was true that my altar-boy side had a hard time grappling with the sexual mores of France, compounded by those of the 1960s, then why did I feel no guilt about my infidelities? Shouldn't I have expressed to Father Burke-Savage a sincere desire to remain true to my marriage, and been absolved by him? Instead, I was almost defiant; surely not the attitude of an Irish Catholic of the old school.

This is where I must admit that, in addition to the social and political tensions that were altering the world around me and also my interior world, there was the fact of my personal history and its affect on my psyche. At the age of four I was forsaken by my mother, a trauma which must have reverberated through the ensuing years of childhood and into my adult life. Finally, after having been abandoned by the one woman who mattered most, I desired, and was desired by, many women, and this multiplicity was comforting, a kind of love insurance.

I also think I was partly wrong when I told Father Burke-Savage that sex was a quicker way truly to know someone else. I have learnt, in the course of my amorous life, that physical intimacy does not automatically lead to emotional intimacy; that the coupling of limbs does not always result in a meeting of minds. In fact, the phrase *post coitum, homo tristis est* can be most true when one has had sex without love or a real knowledge of one's partner, leaving one feeling obscurely lonely. Years later I would write 'Don Juan's Farewell', which opens with the lines:

> Ladies I have lain
>> with in darkened rooms . . .

and concludes:

>> and you slowly awake
> to confront again
>> the alluring lie
> of searching through
>> another's pliant body
> for something missing
>> in your separate self
> while profound night
>> like a black swan
> goes pluming past.

II

OLD MOULDS

Eamonn Gallagher, a friend of long standing in the Irish diplomatic corps, has become Taoiseach Jack Lynch's advisor on
Northern affairs. Lynch is from Cork, which, I am beginning to
realise, is as far away from the North as one can get while still
being in Ireland: a psychic remoteness as well as a merely geographical one. But Gallagher is an abrasive Donegal man, as
hard-headed as they come, and we have had many discussions
on the North over the years, while *The Rough Field*, my long
poem on Ulster, was evolving.

This time, however, we are driving up together from Dublin
in his aged but reliable French banger. Sometimes he stays in the
Wellington Park Hotel, but he meets most of his contacts in the
Europa, Belfast's most heavily guarded hotel fortress, like a
compound in the Middle East. There he meets journalists,
sometimes in that strange cocktail lounge with a racing motif,
horsewhips and hunting caps adorning the walls in a Belfast version of Krafft-Ebbing. And with young barmaids – or perhaps
one should say 'wenches' – displaying their décolleté like scoops
of ice cream.

As well as journalist friends, he meets politicians like John
Hume and Paddy Devlin. (He probably sees paramilitaries occasionally as well, though in more discreet circumstances, like the
privacy of a hotel room.) Off-stage, there is the occasional

rattle of rifle fire, the thud of what may be a muffled explosion. One night in his room, working through the remnants of a bottle of Black Bush, I quote the opening lines of *The Rough Field*: 'Old moulds are broken in the North . . . '. Or did an amused though exhausted Eamonn put these words into my mouth? In either case, he used them as the opening for a famous speech delivered by Jack Lynch on 11 July 1970, which tried to calm the deepening tensions in the North. Thus began that rather noble practice of Irish statesmen, even now including Ian Paisley, of quoting from modern Irish poets. But could poetry heal this opening wound? In composing the speech, Eamonn did not include my second line: 'In the dark streets, firing starts'.

In any case, another aspect of my return to Ireland is that the long poem I have been working on for a decade is nearly complete, several sections having already been published by Dolmen, like 'Patriotic Suite', a bitter-sweet commentary on the fiftieth commemoration of 1916 (which, ironically, had been set up in proofs for *Studies* by my Jesuit friend Father Burke-Savage, though, alas, he did not print it, perhaps because of discreet though powerful Episcopal disapproval?). The Dolmen Press also published 'A New Siege', a poem on Derry dedicated to Bernadette Devlin.

I am also coming North because, at long last, I have younger confrères in Belfast, with whom I can stay: the Heaneys in Ashley Avenue near the university, with the Longleys up the way, and Derek Mahon strolling through Cyril Connolly's 'gardens of the West'. An eager young champion of the arts, called Michael Emmerson, is organising a Belfast Festival, and indeed the young Longley announces to me solemnly that he feels that this new generation of Northern poets will be 'the biggest thing since the poets of the thirties'. (He may be right, but I wonder where that leaves me, a decade older than the lot of them, and a lone voice, as opposed to their dynamic chorus. The

Education Act of 1944 is clearly bearing fruit, although, alas, too late for me, which leaves me beginning to feel a bit like a literary John the Baptist.)

Anyway, the Heaneys and Longleys receive me warmly into this new literary scene, though there are noises off. I remember, most poignantly, one night when Evelyn and I were minding the Heaney children, Michael and Christopher, so as to allow their parents an evening out. At some point, we heard the now dismayingly familiar crackle of gunfire in the distance. The two little boys, their eyes wide with anxiety, appeared in their pyjamas, asking, 'Are the bad men coming?'

Another evening highlights some of the complicated strands of the rapidly changing situation. It is the aftermath of Bloody Sunday in Derry; many of the poets have attended the protest march in Newry: Longley and Heaney from Belfast, Kinsella and myself from the South. (Tom and I have also seen a mob attack the British Embassy in Dublin's elegant Merrion Square, in the process destroying the little Lantern Theatre that stood in the basement, centre for most of our poetry readings.)

Tom has written a baleful denunciation of Bloody Sunday, a broadsheet or broadside called *Butcher's Dozen*, which channels the fury that many felt at the brutality of the 'Paras'. And I have already read my own political-pamphlet poem, 'A New Siege', outside Armagh Gaol, during Bernadette Devlin's holiday there. So not surprisingly, we are asked to a reading in Clonard Monastery in the Ardoyne, at the top of the Falls. The Clonard is a kind of legend in the North: the monks are meant to be very tolerant towards 'hard cases' in the Confessional. On feast days in the summer it is very much a focus for the faithful and, with its fluttering banners, can look like a church festival in Spain.

But now, while the hall is full, the atmosphere is not festive but grim. It is clear that the audience are in no mood for sophisticated banter, or the kind of light-hearted patter that poets use

as an entr'acte to draw people in. What they want is raw emotion, and even the Anglo-Saxon stresses of 'A New Siege' are
not direct enough for such a hungry crowd, while Heaney's historical parallel between the bog burials of Jutland and our fresh
atrocities are greeted with bemused courtesy.

It is only when Kinsella begins to recite the opening lines of
Butcher's Dozen that they come alive. As usual, Tom reads steadi-
ly and carefully, without histrionic flourishes, but his passionate
anger strikes home, especially since the poem had appeared in
the *Irish News*, the nationalist paper of the North, the day before:
Butcher's Dozen, already familiar to some in the crowd, is just the
angry lament that they have been yearning for:

> And when I came where thirteen died
> It shrivelled up my heart. I sighed
> And looked about that brutal place
> Of rage and terror and disgrace.

Tom's wife, Eleanor, is delighted, as though something has
been proven, and afterwards she tackles me for not appreciating
her husband's new poem. Which is indeed partly true, since its
immediacy and bluntness had taken me aback. I had forgotten
Tom's admiration for a neglected English poet, Charles
Churchill, who had lampooned many of his contemporaries
(including Goldsmith) in his octosyllabic broadsides. I had not
realised that *Butcher's Dozen* was another such political broadside
in verse form, bold as a ballad.

As we are leaving, the audience stand to attention for *A
Soldier's Song*. I cannot but notice how many young men, at the
back of the hall, are wearing mackintoshes with suspicious
bulges beneath, like characters in *The Informer*. In subdued mood,
we drive home to Ashley Avenue, through the darkened city.
Seamus, also made a bit distracted by the intensity of the
evening, forgets about the ramps that are meant to slow all

traffic. We strike one with a bump, outside the Andersonstown barracks, and I see a soldier go down on one knee, his rifle at the ready. Seamus slows down and, even more subdued than before, we travel back into the consoling university atmosphere of august stone and leafy avenues.

III

'DR MONTAGUE'

I am in New York to give a few readings, and after I have discharged my literary duties I would like to drop into exhibitions, trawl bookshops and see friends. Only I have just a few days to spare from my teaching obligations in Cork, so I must speed round the city. Also I am short of what my hippie friends call 'bread'. Since time is of the essence, I would like to stay in a place where I would not be burdened with social obligations, but a hotel would swallow my fees. What can I do?

A doctor friend, whom I admire a great deal, offers to put me up in a spare bed in his temporarily empty clinic at an uptown hospital. I admire him because he is a new kind of doctor, aware not only of local but also of international health problems, seeing the wider picture of man struggling in our new world, where prosperity and poverty collide. He also loves art in its many forms, especially contemporary Irish painting and sculpture.

After a busy but happy week tearing through New York, from the Metropolitan Museum of Art to the galleries of SoHo, from the cluttered flats of literary pals to the tidy Queens home of my Aunt Eileen, I say goodbye to my doctor friend. I ask what could I possibly do for him, to express my thanks for his eccentric form of hospitality?

He seems to reflect for a minute, and then surprises me by suggesting, 'Perhaps you could come with me to speak to some patients?'

As I am puzzled, not being a doctor, he explains further: 'But these are special patients, suffering from a new malady that frightens people, a disease no one wants to deal with. Even the hospital staff are scared. They think of it as a kind of plague.'

I am at once fascinated and frightened, but he tells me that it is not contagious in the ordinary way, though the symptoms are so extreme that people do not know how to react. Nurses, even some doctors, are so wary that they refuse to bathe these patients or dress their sores. So they are very lonely as well as sick, ostracised as well as in pain. Compassion wins the day, and I find myself in a white doctor's coat, heading for the ward where these strange people (curiously, all men) are corralled. 'Remember, all you have to do is speak to them, and perhaps shake their hands,' my doctor friend has advised.

'This is Doctor Montague, a distinguished physician from Cork,' he announces (the doctor bit is literally true, though not in the medical sense), as we walk along a line of beds. Yes, they are all men, but damaged men, some mottled with purple sores, one going blind, all fatalistically silent, stricken. We pass along the beds one by one, and engage the men in conversation, for which they are heartbreakingly grateful, smiling and gazing eagerly at us out of their exhausted eyes. I am introduced to a gaunt man who tells me he is writing a play: I say that I have just seen an Edward Albee revival, and intend to see a Eugene O'Neill that evening. He discusses both playwrights and both plays, a sensitive and intelligent man whose face I seem to see through a slowly closing door.

An hour passes, during which some of the men even relax at our fairly normal badinage, probably relieved to be treated as ordinary human beings, albeit human beings in great pain.

Then a clatter, as the nurses burst in, trundling the evening meal on noisy trolleys. They do not put the trays down gently, but thrust them, nearly bounce them, onto the patients' tables. And they do not smooth the pillows or straighten the bedclothes in the usual caring manner of nurses, but rush in and out without a word or even a smile, like bats out of hell.

IV

PRECIOUS LITTLE

I am in Paris for Les Belles Etrangères, the French programme for distinguished foreign writers – Irish this time. And although I am staying in Montparnasse, the scene of most of our meetings, and nocturnal revels, I am reluctant to call on Beckett. His last note said that he was 'in an old crock's home' but hoped to be 'out and about under my own steam and back for the boulevard and fit for company again'. But word is out that he is ill, indeed dying, and I am loath to say goodbye to an old friend of over a quarter of a century's standing. Besides, I have a broken leg, and am barely mobile myself, a 'beautiful stranger' in name only.

But a message comes that he wants to see me, so I hobble and swing over to a *tête de station*, or taxi rank, beside the Dôme, where we have so often sat drinking and talking. Then down Raspail, another of our routes, to the lion statue of Denfert Rochereau. At night he would go left, down Boulevard St Jacques, as I turned into my home in the Rue Daguerre, with 'God bless' as his last, uncanny salutation, a familiar Irish phrase made strange by his worldwide reputation for godlessness.

The clinic is in a side street off Avenue du General LeClerc, up which the French general led his liberating troops. And his room is on the ground floor, easily accessible for even the one-legged. A few patients are resting on the courtyard, under winter trees, a tranquil, enclosed setting. I find the door of 'Monsieur Beckett' without difficulty, knock, and swing in.

Beckett is sitting in a bare room at one of two small desks, with a stark iron bed behind. He rises to embrace me, kissing me, to my surprise, on both cheeks; he is not usually so demonstrative.

'Ah, John. You managed it.'

The eyes are watery, but briefly, almost defiantly, bright, as they focus and almost smile.

'It was so good of you to come. And you bad yourself. How's the leg?'

And as I falter a few inconsequential, deprecatory details, he starts to shuffle around. From the familiar, angular athleticism of even his seventies, he is now slowed – slowed considerably – to the dragging gait of one of his own characters. But he is intent on finding a chair for me to sit at his side. We tug it into place together, and there we are, face to face, as often before.

'And how are you?' I ask.

'I'm done.'

A phrase I have not heard since my Aunt Mary lay dying, but the Irishism comes as naturally to Beckett as to that old country lady. And again the eyes focus on me, and I am astounded as always by their size and colour, large as blue marbles. But clouded now, not watchful or challenging.

'I'm done', again, with the same vehemence. 'But it takes such a long time.'

He pauses and draws a breath. He suffers from his lungs, and there is a breathing machine in the corner like a small trolley, with cylinders.

'I sat beside my father when he was dying. "Fight, fight, fight," he kept saying. But I have no fight left.'

A gesture of resignation and, perhaps, disappointment. So far, our conversation has been uncharacteristically circumspect, even stilted, but now, sensing an opening, I feel brave enough for a direct, personal question, even without the ritual glass before me.

'And now that it's nearly over, Sam, can I ask you, was there much of the journey you found worthwhile?'

The blue eyes briefly ignite. 'Precious little.' And in case I did not hear or comprehend, he repeats it again with redoubled force, 'Precious little', and adds, 'For bad measure, I watched both my parents die.'

The 'both' is emphasised, fiercely. But then a thought strikes him and, as if to contradict his own natural, now-justified gloom, he directs us towards his second-best desk, collecting a bottle of whiskey and glasses as he goes.

'Now that you're here, there's a job to be done.' He settles into the second desk seat and, with surprising vigour, empties out a cylinder marked 'Poetry Ireland'. Curling vellum pages, a small black ink bottle, a long slender pen, and a covering letter.

'This man Dorgan, is he all right?' he asks peremptorily.

As I struggle to explain the many qualities of my former student, now a well-known Irish writer and broadcaster, Beckett cuts me short, and points to the official notepaper of Poetry Ireland, of which I am president.

'He must be all right: your name's on the masthead.'

I read with him over his shoulder: it is the 'Great Book of Ireland' project, a lavish compendium of the poets and artists of Ireland, which Dorgan hopes will subsidise Irish poetry till the end of time. Now Beckett pulls a blank page towards him, but the scroll will not stay put. Baffled, he wrestles with the vellum, whilst I set up the small black ink bottle, with the skinny nib to dip in it, nearby. Finally, I have to hold down the curling corners of the paper, as he strives to write what may well be his last lines. They are not new; he has chosen a quatrain written after his

236

father's death, and the implications for his own demise, so long attended, are all too clear:

> redeem the surrogate goodbyes
> the sheet astream in your hand
> who have no more for the land
> and the glass unmisted above your eyes

The sheet is not astream, but bucking and bounding, and his hands are shaking. Twice he has to stroke out lines, but he still goes on, with that near-ferocity I associate with him, until the four lines are copied, in the centre of a page. He looks at me, I look down to check, and murmur appropriate approval. He rolls the vellum and, with due ceremony, hands it over to me, with the carton. Then, with a gesture of finality that brooks no contradiction (so much for the manuscript collections of the world!), he sweeps the lot – ink bottle, long black pen, and spare pages of vellum – into the waste-paper bin.

Job done, we rest a while, glass in hand. He shows me the books he has been reading, old favourites, *The Oxford Book of French Verse*, which he probably studied at Trinity College under his beloved Rudnose Brown, who introduced him to contemporary French literature. And *The Penguin Book of English Verse*, with a few later volumes of his own and, to my embarrassment, my recent book of essays, *The Figure in the Cave*, incongruously wedged between.

'I've been reading Keats's "Ode to a Nightingale". It's very beautiful.'

It happens to be a poem that I nearly dislike, because of its association with exams, but this is not the time for sparring matches, even if fuelled by Jameson. His barriers are down, his sympathies simple; he has gone back to the pleasant discoveries of boyhood. I reflect instead that I have never heard him use the word 'beautiful' before, except in connection with Yeats. I mention that to him, and he nods. 'Ah, yes, yes, beautiful, too.'

He will not let me pour, but sloshes more whiskey into our glasses. 'I got your new book. I see you mention me. And Goldsmith. Ah, he was a nice man. I liked what you said about me. The writing is good.'

I don't dare ask more, but do mention something that has troubled me, a recent rumour. 'Is it true that you are dictating something about yourself, something autobiographical?'

He rears back. 'Oh, no, nothing like that, just tidying up the letters. Getting things straight. Only the professional details, nothing personal.'

But the note has been struck, and I sound it again. 'And where do you want to be, when you go?'

'Ah, next door, in Montparnasse. With the wife. We knew each other for fifty years. We played tennis together when we met, and, after the stabbing, she came back. Ah, yes, with the wife. We were friends for fifty years.'

'Friends' stands out; he does not say, 'We loved each other for fifty years', or suchlike. Perhaps it is a translation of the French all-purpose word *ami*? Shall I quiz him about love and friendship, as I have sometimes done in the past? In our previous meeting, we had discussed the death of an old friend, Con (A. J.) Leventhal, who, after a long and pleasure-loving life, had turned his face to the wall. When I mentioned how much he was liked by the ladies, Beckett had said, admiringly, 'He certainly had a lot of them', as if speaking of a stable of horses. But I keep to the present.

'Who's looking after things, the other things?'

'Edward, the nephew: he's very good. He's in the flat at the moment. He'll do everything that has to be done. Would you have another drink?'

There is no drink left: although I did not measure the spirit level, we seem to have cleared the remnants of that bottle, as often before. I rise to help, but he waves me down, shuffling across the room again, a speeding snail, to a cupboard which seems chock-a-block with bottles. Indeed, I have rarely seen so many bottles outside a wakehouse: whiskey, the Irishman's morphine. He tugs across a litre bottle of Bushmills Malt, clearly a gift from an unknown benefactor.

And a benefactor it is, because, for once, I feel totally at ease with Sam, stocious and glorious, as though something had been completed. Side by side, we sit, for what is clearly the last time. We discuss what I am over for, Les Belles Etrangères, and he gives me a commission for Jack Lang, the Minister for Culture, to whom he feels he owes a favour, done for his niece, Caroline. Beckett, the family man. I'm impressed, as always, by his (Protestant?) punctiliousness.

And then, to my astonishment, he tries a stave of an old Protestant hymn. 'Do you know that one?' he asks. I try to join in, in catholic good fellowship, but lack of familiarity with the words does not help my share of the duet. It is not 'Rock of Ages', or Cardinal Newman's 'Lead Kindly Light', so incongruously sung by the Protestant Miss Fitt in *All That Fall*, but the gloomy lines of Baring-Gould, beloved also of Auden. When the words grind to a halt, we grin at each other and try again:

> Now the day is over
> Night is drawing nigh
> Shadows of the evening
> Steal across the sky.

And then I realise: it is of course the hymn quoted in *Watt*. And indeed it is time to go: we have been most of the afternoon together. I help him to tidy the desk, arrange his books. He stands up, to embrace me on both cheeks for the second time. Those flaring jug ears; that furrowed brow above staring seagull's eyes; the limbre spare body, now slowed by time: I will never see it, or him, again. He presses a last present, the texts gathered in *Teleplays*, into my left hand; the carton is suspended from my right crutch. We do not discuss a further meeting, as I swing out the door. In this side street, a taxi will be hard to find.

The publishers gratefully acknowledge the following for granting permission to reproduce copyright material: 'Burning 12' by Gary Snyder, from *Myths and Texts*, copyright ©1978 by Gary Snyder. Reprinted by permission of New Directions Publishing Corp. 'I Feel Like I'm Fixin' To Die Rag' words and music written by Joe Macdonald. Published by Chrysalis Music © 1967. Used by permission. All rights reserved. The lines from 'Personal Problem' by Patrick Kavanagh are reprinted from *Collected Poems*, edited by Antoinette Quinn (Allen Lane, 2004) by kind permission of the Trustees of the Estate of the late Katherine B. Kavanagh, through the Jonathan Williams Literary Agency. The lines from 'Butchers Dozen' by Thomas Kinsella are reprinted from *Collected Poems* (Carcanet Press, 2000). The lines from *Dream Songs* by John Berryman are reprinted by permission of Faber & Faber Ltd. The front-cover image, *Liberty on the Barricades (After Delacroix)* by Robert Ballagh, is reproduced by kind permission of the artist and the Irish Museum of Modern Art. The publishers have made every effort to trace holders of copyright material and would be happy to amend any oversights in this regard in future printings of the book.